Implementing Juran's road
map for quality leadership

IMPLEMENTING JURAN'S ROAD MAP FOR QUALITY LEADERSHIP

IMPLEMENTING JURAN'S ROAD MAP FOR QUALITY LEADERSHIP

Benchmarks and Results

AL ENDRES

John Wiley & Sons, Inc.

New York • Chichester • Weinheim • Brisbane • Singapore • Toronto

This publication is designed to provide accurate and authoritative
information in regard to the subject matter covered. It is sold with the
understanding that the publisher is not engaged in rendering legal,
accounting, or other professional services. If legal advice or other expert
assistance is required, the services of a competent professional person
should be sought.

Library of Congress Cataloging-in-Publication Data:

Endres, Al C., 1942–
    Implementing Juran's road map for quality leadership : benchmarks
    and results / Al Endres.
        p.   cm.
    Includes bibliographical references and index.
    ISBN 0-471-29619-8 (cloth : alk. paper)
    1. Total quality management.   I. Juran Institute.   II. Title.
    HD62.15.E534   2000
    658.4'013—dc21   99-29528

Printed in the United States of America.

10   9   8   7   6   5   4   3   2   1

This book is dedicated to my mother and father,
LaRayne and Alphonse,
who started and supported the initial phases of my life's journey.
It is also dedicated to
Diane and Alyson, my wife and daughter,
who have been the rewards for expanding the journey's scope.

Contents

Foreword

For years we have been observing a great number of the best and brightest thinkers in achieving business excellence during presentations at Juran Institute's annual IMPRO conferences. The carefully selected executives from leading companies in numerous countries frequently surprise us by the creativity and innovativeness many of these companies demonstrate in solving problems, creating new products, and reducing cycle times. One of the continuing surprises is the magnitude of many of the improvements. Managers used to striving for incremental improvements of 5 or 10 percent are often stunned to hear of 90 percent reductions in defects, of cycle times being cut by 30, 50, or even 80 percent, and of new products being launched defect free.

It was during these conferences we first heard of quality improvement projects that spanned company boundaries. What then was revolutionary has now become common place among the best managed organizations. We first saw the quality improvement storyboard in the early 1980s, a tool that was quickly adopted in Japan and has become a mainstay of their continuing quality control circle activities. We heard chief finance officers tell of being pushed by their CEOs to apply the same methods so successfully used in manufacturing processes to drastically cut the time to close books, write contracts, and share best practices during audits rather than just finding variations.

We heard directors of major research labs tell of break-throughs in design practices, dramatic reductions in patent application times, and new means for capturing customer needs and desires. We learned that the same methods used for break-throughs in manufacturing quality could be applied to transactional processes. Long before the word *reengineering* was coined, we heard of stunning successes in reducing proposal times, decreasing account receivables by over 50 percent, and in simplifying inventory management. We heard about orders taken in the field transmitted directly to factory assemblers who had completed the entire production within minutes of the customer explaining exactly what was needed.

These success stories came from all over the world and from every industry. At first we were surprised by the commonality of the problems. Whether the speakers were from Italy, the United Kingdom, Brazil, Japan, Malaysia, or the United States, they were describing the same problems. Some speakers came from high-tech industries that produced cellular phones, consumer electronics, and computers. Others came from telecommunications, aerospace, oil and gas, and automotive companies. Still others came from railroads, hotels, rental car companies, health care providers, medical devices manufacturers, and the food processing industry. Still later we started seeing speakers and participants from all branches of government service including the Air Force, Army, Coast Guard, and Navy. We soon realized that the problems facing organizations were remarkably similar whether in highly-competitive industries, government service, or health care. We quickly discovered that the answers to these problems took many different forms, but these solutions were quickly adapted, modified, and applied across organizations, industries, and countries.

Until now, no one has taken the time to plow through 15 years of these varied experiences and this extensive wealth of lessons learned to delve into the common factors of success or the universal truths contained in the stories from such a wide-ranging and varied body of work. Dr. A.C. Endres has undertaken this daunting task and created a remarkable body of work. By searching for the common themes, similar approaches, and significant results, Al has created a text, a reference book, and a guide for all managers. This resulting work should be studied by all executives, managers, and professionals for the concepts, methods and tools used by some of the most successful companies and organizations in the world.

These lessons come from CEOs and presidents, executives, and managers of many of the outstanding companies in the world. They come from generals, admirals, ministers, and other highly-ranked government employees. But they also come from factory workers, clerks, sergeants, and maintenance employees. These conferences were begun by the driving force of Motorola, which early on, had the idea that by sharing their experiences they could entice others to share. And this sharing would enable all to learn faster. Many of the company names are familiar: AT&T, Toyota, General Motors, Royal Dutch Shell/Shell International, Boeing, Cessna, Electrolux A.B, British Telcom, GTE, Southern Pacific, Milliken and Company, Florida Power and Light, Xerox, Olivetti, Nokia, Motorola, General Electric, Texas Instruments, Alcoa, Mayo Clinic, Kaiser Permanente, Duracell, and Ford.

But there are also many small companies in the mix, many of which are unknown outside of their industries. Many of the larger companies were surprised by how much they had to learn from companies a hundredth or thousandth of their size. We found that many of these small companies, such as Ames, SØL, and Globe Metallurgical, were able to move faster, change quicker, and achieve striking results. The methods they used were similar but applied with great enthusiasm and other twists. We learned much from these companies.

In this text, we can find a great deal about the history of the quality movement in the United States and the world. We are able to see the shift from quality improvement projects to total quality management. Later, we note the beginnings of strategic quality planning and deployment. We witness the shift from quality initiatives to business and performance excellence. Looking closely we can observe the start of many of the future trends, the new ideas that are beginning to shape business today—and in the next century.

We are recognizing many of these ideas incorporated in the Six Sigma/Black Belt quality movement. Created by Motorola in the 1980s and extended recently by AlliedSignal, General Electric, and others, we are now observing how leaders can drive goals and stunning financial results throughout all areas of an organization by using the concepts, methods, and tools developed over the past 15 years. Companies are now using full-time team leaders and analysts to tackle the hardest, most rewarding problems and opportunities. They are providing intensive training in the most useful of the methods and tools and incorporating these tools in easy-to-use software. They are extending their support to both customers and key suppliers—true business partners. These methods are continually driving down costs and strengthening competitive positions and profits.

We are seeing new breakthroughs in understanding customer needs and wants, often long before the customers themselves realize these needs. We are watching organizations move beyond "must-have quality" to the "attractive quality" that creates new customers, new markets, and new product lines. These ideas create strong competitive positions for many of these companies.

We are observing an almost fanatical concentration on speed. Quick times to market has become a necessity rather than a competitive advantage. Reduced cycle times and just-in-time manufacturing have been added to just-in-time inventory cycles to create a supply-chain management philosophy that is revolutionizing manufacturing and service businesses.

We are living in truly interesting times. Every day we hear new predictions of how the Internet will have an impact on business greater than the industrial revolution. New business models are being created every day. We now have production capacities in many industries and parts of the world that far exceed demands. As Joseph M. Juran has often said, the twentieth century will be remembered as the century of productivity, but the twenty-first will surely be the century of quality. Dr. Endres has given us an excellent guide to this new century.

Dr. A. Blanton Godfrey
Chairman and CEO
Juran Institute, Inc.

Preface

The first time I spoke to Dr. Juran I was a senior operations research analyst in Motorola's Communications Products Division in Schaumburg, Illinois. Our division general manager, sensing the swell of momentum for quality improvement launched by Motorola's chairman, Bob Galvin, had asked our director to conduct a study on where the division really stood on quality.

After being given the assignment of determining how to accomplish this daunting task, I called for "reinforcements." I was somewhat surprised, if not startled, when Dr. Juran personally answered his phone with his famous "Juran!" I asked if he were available to help us conduct what I would later learn to call an assessment of quality. Unfortunately, he was not, but he generously suggested several other consultants who could help us.

From the list of consultants he suggested, Ed Reynolds, a seasoned quality professional who told it like it was—even if people didn't want to hear it—was our "best fit." It was while working and learning from Ed, that I made the decision to put aside operations research in favor of a career focused on utilizing and teaching Dr. Juran's concepts and methodologies to help organizations manage for quality.

Approximately 12 years (and two employers) later, I responded to a position announcement in *The Wall Street Journal* for "Quality Professionals" at Juran Institute. My first interview for that position was with Dr. Juran. A key concept that he required me to explain was my perception of the primary *differences* among Crosby's, Deming's, and Juran's approaches to managing quality. I responded that I believed Crosby had made valuable contributions in building senior managers' awareness of opportunities for cost reduction by introducing the price of nonconformance. I believed that Deming had demonstrated the benefits derivable from using statistical process control (SPC), and had provided broad guidelines for developing a quality culture. However, I believed Juran had provided a more comprehensive explanation of the *structure and processes* required for answering the question: *How do we get there from here?*

Although my answers were not perfect, they were apparently good enough to receive an offer of employment, which I eagerly accepted. Subsequently, I was asked to participate, with other Institute quality professionals, in reviewing a typical sequence of phases and activities that had been found useful in helping our customers' organizations plan (and review) their quality initiatives. A task force led by John Early significantly enhanced an early version of a Road Map developed by Frank Gryna that was focused on implementing Juran's Quality Improvement process for chronic quality problems. The results of that task force and other comments at the Juran Institute became known as The Road Map.

The Road Map is the basis for this book. Examples of its use were taken from the reports of the leaders and managers responsible for transforming the concepts into reality. This book has greatly benefited from their decisions to share their experiences. Their experiences were presented at Juran Institute's IMPRO conferences and associated proceedings.

Locating what I considered to be the right example to demonstrate a particular phase or activity within the Road Map was made immeasurably easier by the availability of a searchable CD ROM of IMPRO proceedings developed by Arturo Onias and TPOK in cooperation with the Juran Institute.

University of Tampa　　　　　　　　Al Endres
August 1999　　　　　　　　　　*Director, Center for Quality*

IMPLEMENTING JURAN'S ROAD MAP FOR QUALITY LEADERSHIP

CHAPTER I

Accelerating Performance through Quality

Performance Improvement: Drivers and Challenges

Today's organizations (manufacturing, service, and government) are seeking not only to improve their performance by becoming more efficient, but want to become more efficient more *quickly*. The primary drivers for accelerating performance improvements are:

1. Intensified global competition.

2. Increased sophistication and demands of customers (higher expectations for features, and lower tolerances of deficiencies).

3. Increased employee job mobility.

4. Rapid changes in technology (e.g., Intranets drastically shortening new-product development cycles).

In this chapter, we review some of the more frequent responses to the need for increased performance improvement and identify the primary reasons for their successes and failures. Understanding the reasons, concepts, processes, and tools required to manage for quality is necessary to help other organizations benefit from past experiences and best practices.

Juran (1993) provided a striking example of the need to accelerate improvements. Although the quality of American automobiles *was* improving, it was not improving *quickly enough* to ensure long-term survival (Figure 1.1). Only after the American automobile industry seriously adopted many of the concepts that will be discussed, was it able to accelerate improvement and subsequently survive the onslaught of international competition. In reporting on GM's strategy to focus its assembly plants on larger assemblies versus components, Bradshaw (1998) stated: "The

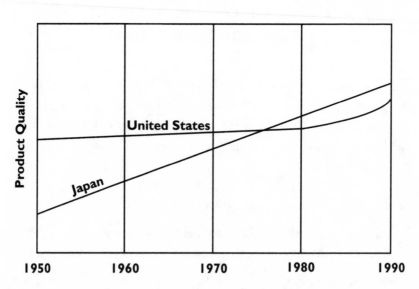

Figure 1.1 Japan vs. United States: Improvements in Automobile Quality.

company's (GM's) biggest problem is that every time it seems to be catching up with the rest of industry, other automakers make further progress themselves."

A key determinant of long-term market success is the *rate* of improvement versus competitors. Coletti (1994) provided an example of the results obtainable from "accelerating" the design and development of Ford's new Mustang. Because of improvements in the product development process, Ford's redesigned Mustang arrived in dealers' showrooms in 25 percent less time, with 30 percent less capital spending ($300 million), and 40 percent less staffing, while simultaneously attaining a 15 percent increase in customer satisfaction. Statistics like these remind us that quality is a pathway, not the final destination. The efficacy of any organizational initiative must always be judged on the results it achieves, that is, the benefits derived from the responses it stimulates.

Partial Responses

Examples of recent partial responses by organizations have included:

1. Developing and communicating visions and strategies.

2. Reengineering.

3. ISO 9000.

4. Employee empowerment (including self-directed work teams).

Vision and strategy are necessary for defining, respectively, where an organization wishes to go and how it wishes to get there. However, organizations must be able to successfully *align*, *implement*, and *manage* their visions and strategies with their processes and their employees. David Norton, president of Renaissance Solutions, and codeveloper (with Robert Kaplan) of the Balanced Score Card concept, has stated: "Less than 10 percent of strategies effectively formulated are effectively executed" (*Fortune*, 1997). Similarly, Norton cites the CSC Index organization statistic that "67 percent of reengineering efforts achieve marginal to no results at all."

Although ISO 9000 registration is desirable, is it not sufficient to drive performance *improvement*. Reiman and Hertz (1993) of the Office of Quality Programs at the U.S. National Institute of Standards and Technology (NIST) stated: "The focus of ISO 9000 registration is *conformity* to practices specified in the registrant's own quality systems—factors not addressed in ISO 9000 registration or addressed differently (from the Baldrige criteria)—include: customer and market focus; results orientation; continuous improvement; competitive comparisons; tie to business strategy; cycle time and responsiveness; integration via analysis; public responsibility; human resource development; and information sharing."

Empowering employees to implement their organization's strategy *can* unleash an enormous amount of potential energy. However, if managers don't align the employees' goals with the organization's strategy, at best they produce "random acts of improvement." Employees must be provided with the tools they need to meet their goals. If employees can't regulate their performance within the processes in which they must work, they are more likely to become exasperated than energized. Rocca (1991) of IBM Rochester has stated that before employees can be empowered, they must first be enabled; after they see their results, they become energized.

Whitaker (1995), at Eastman Chemical, another Baldrige award winner, provided an integrated perspective:

Within every organization lies the key resource to effectively compete in the global marketplace—its people. Regardless of an organization's position on the quality journey, the ultimate challenge is to maintain an environment that enables every employee to contribute at his/her fullest potential. The people asset appreciates in value throughout the quality journey; however, its fullest potential has yet to be realized.

A more comprehensive framework is needed if the organization is to implement and then assess the results of its strategy.

Comprehensive Responses and Their Results

To facilitate understanding the *infrastructure* required to develop and manage organizational performance, the Baldrige Criteria (1999) provide a system's perspective of the drivers for organization performance. Juran (1993) referred to the Baldrige Award and the dissemination of its criteria for performance excellence as one of the primary drivers for accelerating an organization's pace of quality improvement. Figure 1.2, from *Criteria for Performance Excellence* (1999), depicts the interrelationships that must be constructed for driving business results through managing for quality.

Indicators for the results gleaned by organizations that have developed and deployed the necessary infrastructure for operationalizing the Baldrige system's perspective have been summarized by the National Institute of Standards and Technology (NIST, 1999). NIST has constructed and tracked a "Baldrige Index—made up of six publicly-traded U.S. companies that

Figure 1.2   The Systems View of the Baldrige Categories' Linkages.

received the Malcolm Baldrige National Quality Award during the years 1988–1997. . . . NIST found that the group of six out-performed the Standard & Poor's 500 (Stock Index) by more than 2.6 to 1, achieving a 460 percent return on investment compared to a 175 percent return for S&P 500."*

Figure 1.3, from Juran Institute's IMPRO conference, shows a similar business management model used by Xerox to help implement its Leadership Through Quality initiative. (Additional material on Xerox's Strategic Planning Process is in Chapter 6.)

By successfully implementing the infrastructure for the system's model, two of Xerox's businesses won "Baldies." In 1989, the Business Products and Systems (BP&S) business unit received the Baldrige Quality Award for its demonstration of breakthrough results. BP&S reduced the number of defects per copy machine by 78 percent, decreased unscheduled machine maintenance by 40 percent, and reduced service response times by 27 percent (NIST Web Site, 1998). In 1997, Xerox's Business Services (XBS) division captured a "Baldie" for providing outstanding document

---

* For additional information on the exact process used to calculate the index, contact NIST at http://www.quality.nist.gov/.

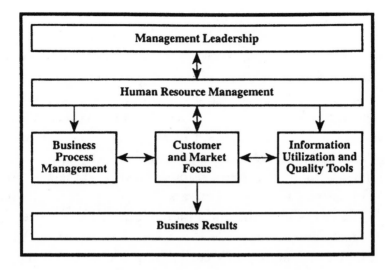

Figure 1.3 The Xerox Management Model (Leo, 1994).

outsourcing and consulting services to businesses worldwide. XBS leads its competitors in overall customer satisfaction and is a benchmark in 7 of 10 drivers for customer satisfaction. During the previous five years, revenues and profits increased by 30 percent per year, and XBS attained a 40 percent market share—"nearly three times the share of its nearest competitor."

Concepts Required for Managing Quality

To accelerate the achievement of such results, upper managers must understand how to think about quality and their responsibilities in leading quality revolutions. Juran (1993) stated: "In 1954, I gave the Japanese the same quality lectures I'd been giving here at home. But in Japan, it was the CEOs who listened." A key determinant of an organization's success in implementing a comprehensive quality initiative is a common understanding of how to think about quality. A general definition was provided by Juran and Gryna (1993), who defined quality goods and services as those that are "Fit for use." Juran (1992) suggested that "fitness for use" should be determined from two primary dimensions: (1) product features and (2) freedom from deficiencies (Table 1.1). *Product features* are inherent product properties that are intended to meet certain customer needs, and thereby result in customer satisfaction and increased revenues but often result in higher costs. The other dimension, *product deficiencies* results in product failures that produce customer dissatisfaction. When done correctly, lowering deficiencies will produce lower costs and lower cycle times.

Table 1.1   The Two Dimensions of Quality

Product Features

- Respond to customer needs.
- Compete for market share.
- Create product salability.
- Provide product satisfaction.
- Effect is on sales income.
- Higher quality costs more.

Freedom from Deficiencies

- Avoid product dissatisfaction.
- Effect is on cost.
- Higher quality costs less.

Source: © Juran Institute, Inc.

A Model for Managing Quality

Results are driven by an organization's leaders' aligning an organization's human resources, processes, measurements, and information with its strategy (Figure 1.2). This is accomplished by building the necessary structure and processes to align and support the attainment of these requirements (Figure 1.4). We'll now discuss the elements that are the major building blocks of Total Quality Management (TQM). Case examples are integrated throughout subsequent chapters.

FOUNDATION ELEMENTS

The foundation elements for TQM are Customer Focus, Executive Leadership, and Strategic Quality Management (see Figure 1.5).

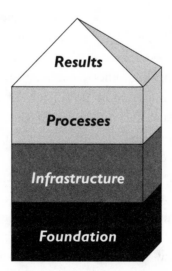

Figure 1.4 Juran Institute's Model for Total Quality Management (TQM)—Macro View.

FOUNDATION

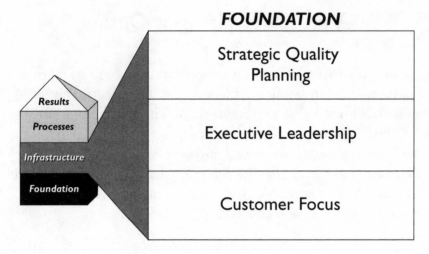

Figure 1.5   The Foundation Elements of TQM.

Customer Focus

The bedrock of the pyramid is *customer focus.* Juran (1995) referred to customer focus as a "core strategy" adopted by organizations that serve as role models for world-class quality. To successfully focus on customers, each organization must adopt and communicate a common definition of a customer. Juran (1992) defined a customer as "anyone who is impacted by the product or process. Customers may be external or internal." To understand and meet the needs of external customers, organizations must know the needs of the end benefactors of its goods and services, as well as understand what its internal customers need, in order to fulfill the needs of the external benefactors. Customer focus is closely tied to both Category 3 (*Customer and Market Focus*) and Category 5 (*Human Resource Focus*) of the Baldrige criteria. Table 1.2 provides some examples of internal suppliers, their products, and their customers.

Table 1.2 Departments and Their Internal Customers

Supplying Departments	Major Products	Internal Customers
Finance	Financial statements	Managers
Employment	Recruits	All departments
Order editing	Edited orders	Operations
Office services	Office space supplies and maintenance	All office departments
Legal	Legal advice	All departments

Source: © Juran Institute, Inc.

Executive Leadership

The second component of the foundation for successful TQM is *Executive Leadership*. Fuchs and Wyndrum (1995), at AT&T Bell Laboratories, reported that "few companies have succeeded in rising to superior levels of performance. . . . There are only a few root causes for their difficulties, not the least of which is the ineffective roles of leaders of the enterprises." Before executives can lead, they must understand their specific roles and responsibilities for leading a quality revolution. Table 1.3 provides a checklist of these responsibilities for use by senior managers and chief quality officers (see Juran, 1995, and Juran and Gryna, 1993). Executive leadership closely ties to Category 1 *(Leadership System)* of the Baldrige criteria.

Knowing and understanding this checklist is helpful, but implementing it is what drives results. Robert Waller, President and Chief Executive Officer of the Mayo Foundation, reported (1996): "I have no special wisdom about leadership; . . . I learned more about quality initiatives as a member of the On-Time Start Team than at all the committee meetings we held on quality put together. This team, dedicated to improving start times in the

Table 1.3 Deeds for Upper Managers in Leading a Quality Revolution

- Serve on quality council.
- Approve strategic quality goals.
- Allocate needed resources.
- Review progress.
- Give recognition.
- Serve on some project teams.
- Revise merit rating system.

Source: © Juran Institute, Inc.

surgical suites, met weekly at 6 A.M. We were led by Pat Strom, a superb surgical nurse, who urged me not to be late for the meetings. I learned that much of the leadership that is needed to facilitate quality improvement cannot be delegated."

Strategic Quality Management

Once an organization has established its vision, mission, and critical success factors (what do we wish to become, why are we here, what must we do to fulfill our mission), it must develop a strategy to determine how it is to achieve its goals. The role of strategic planning within the Baldrige framework is depicted in Figure 1.2. A key dimension of an organization must be its strategy for improving quality. Juran (1992) defined Strategic Quality Management (SQM) as "a structured process for establishing long-range quality goals, at the highest level of the organization, and defining the means to be used to reach those goals." For example, at General Electric, Jack Welch (1998) is using a Six

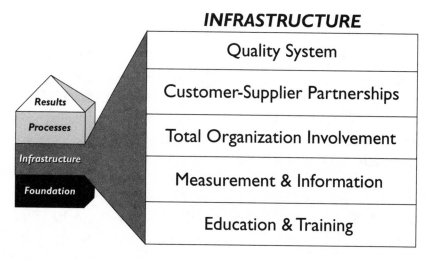

Figure 1.6 Elements of Infrastructure.

Sigma* quality strategy to drive improvement in processes, which, in turn, improves GE's operating margins. (Six Sigma returned)—"more than three quarters of a billion dollars in savings beyond our investment in 1998, with a billion and a half in sight for 1999."

INFRASTRUCTURE ELEMENTS

Figure 1.6 lists the key components of the infrastructure required to perpetuate Total Quality Management.

---

* A process operating at a Six Sigma quality level is expected to yield, in the long term, 3.4 errors per million transactions. Six Sigma at GE was adopted from Motorola and Allied Signal. For more information on Six Sigma, see, M. Harry (1998), "Six Sigma: A Breakthrough Strategy for Profitability," *Quality Progress*, May 1998.

Education and Training

Training and *Education* are key components of the TQM infrastructure. As early as 1966, in an address to a European conference on quality, Juran stated: "The Japanese are headed for world-class quality leadership and will attain it in the next two decades because no one else is moving there at the same pace." Although this initial warning went unheeded, when the success of the Japanese automobiles became apparent in the 1980s, Juran was repeatedly asked to explain this "miracle." Juran's explanations (1981, 1990, 1993) consistently included an emphasis on training and education in the concepts, processes, and tools required to manage for quality. For example, in his 1990 presentation at the "Quest for Excellence" conference, which featured the 1989 winners of the Baldrige Award, Juran stated: "To meet that crisis, the Japanese did many things, but in my view there were three major success factors:

1. The upper managers took charge of solving the quality crisis.

2. They undertook to train the entire managerial hierarchy in how to manage for quality, *starting at the top*.

3. They undertook quality improvement at a revolutionary pace.

Juran (1981) stated that "Upper managers should by all means become trainees in the program. Their training will be partly 'by the book' and partly by the extent to which they participate in the leadership of the quality function." Among the organizations reporting on lessons learned from developing and implementing their training strategies are Carolina Power & Light Company (Leak, 1988), GTE (Murphy, 1988), and Xerox (Palermo and Watson, 1993). Among the lessons reported were:

1. Train "top-down."

2. Select and certify managers to train their workgroups.

3. Tailor the training materials for the group receiving the training.

4. Train "just-in time," not "just-in case."

5. Tie the training to concurrent or follow-on requirements for actions using the materials.

6. Assess the efficacy of the training from its use and results.

These conclusions and recommendations were not restricted to training for quality in the United States. In Sweden, Sandholm (1992) stated: "Training in quality must begin at the top and then pour its way down through the whole organization." Similarly, at Short Brothers PLC, a 9,000-employee designer and manufacturer of aircraft in Belfast, Northern Ireland, Ambrose (1990) reported that, "[since 1987] our training program was very definitely a 'top-down' process starting with the Managing Director and his Board and moving systematically through the company until all personnel were trained." In 1992, Ambrose reported that "we can reflect on some tremendous breakthroughs and look upon over ($40 million) in documented savings."

Measurement and Information

Too many organizations can be characterized as DRIPs (Data Rich and Information Poor). Without the proper data, analysis, and information, organizations do not know where to focus, what to analyze, how to remedy, and what progress they are making. Figure 1.7 provides a pyramid for defining, developing, and aligning measures for all levels of an organization.

The pyramid is useful for envisioning how implementing the infrastructure for TQM will have the concomitant benefit of developing the necessary measures and information for accelerating performance improvement. This pyramid contains several elements (e.g., Strategic Quality Planning) of TQM infrastructure that were previously discussed. Others will be discussed and exemplified later.

Total Organization Involvement

Implementing the elements of TQM will, by definition, help drive involvement from the "board room to the boiler room." The vital role for upper managers has been discussed. This section will address the roles for middle managers and for the workforce.

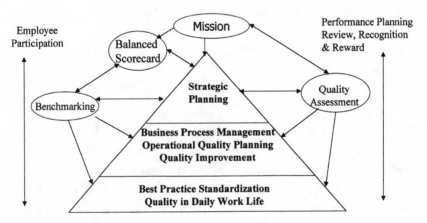

Figure 1.7 A Pyramid for Aligning Quality Measurement and Information.

Middle Managers   It is particularly crucial to secure the involvement of middle managers. Zachman (1990) discussed the strategy used to implement a quality process within AT&T's Chief Financial Officer's organization: "Total employee involvement, the third key element of achieving full mobilization for meeting customer requirements, would be facilitated and supported by middle managers after the latter had been involved personally in the quality process. This would consist of involvement in quality planning efforts on both a team and individual basis (e.g., recognition of customers and suppliers associated with one's job, etc.). It was anticipated this approach would delay getting all employees involved, but provide a much more supportive environment when it did happen."

Endres (1997) stated that middle managers' support is required for:

1. Serving on task forces for developing plans and procedures for the total quality initiative and elements of quality infrastructure.

2. Nominating projects (pilot and follow-on).

3. Screening project nominations.

4. Participating on quality teams.

5. Supporting their employees' training and participation on cross-functional teams.

Because middle managers often represent the largest source of resistance to quality initiatives,* obtaining and rewarding their input and participation are essential to the success of any quality

---

* Main (1994), in *Quality Wars*, has a section entitled "The Forgotten Player: The Middle Manager," which provides lessons learned from Southern Pacific Railroad and Motorola, which, respectively, excluded and included managers in their quality initiatives.

initiative. Middle management support can be obtained through several strategies, including:

1. Start with volunteers.

2. Select pilot projects that will provide visible benefits to middle managers.

3. Recognize and reward exemplary participation and support.

4. Mandate participation as a required element of job responsibility.

The Workforce The American workforce has been one of our business organizations' most underutilized assets. Some of the earlier attempts at involving employees to improve their processes' performance were born from poorly conceived benchmarking visits to Japan. Many managers who made these "industrial tourism" visits observed that Japanese workers were formed into Quality Circles. The visiting managers incorrectly concluded that the circles must be the secret to Japan's increased competitiveness. Unfortunately, they did not realize that the circles were formed only after the support processes were available to "push" the chronic cross-departmental problems uncovered by the circles up to middle and senior management. Predictably, without the necessary support from middle and upper managers, QCs in the United States took off like rockets and came down like rocks. Some examples of these ill-fated attempts in both the United States and Europe were reported by Cornish (1988) of NCR: "As we read about the Japanese methods, we discovered that Quality Circles were one of the innovations they used to make improvements. If it worked for them, it should work for us. We therefore sent a Quality Engineer to learn about Quality Circles and be a Facilitator. We then set up a training program, established a number of Quality Circles, and prepared to reap significant new gains in our quality levels. Over a period of about a year and a half, we had much activity but little quality improvement. We were still using our conventional approach to quality but were disappointed that the Circles weren't meeting our expectations and making their contribution to improvement." Similarly, in Norway, Ole Andreas (1992) reported from *Det Norske Veritas,* "Some years back we had a number of Quality Circles going. Looking upon this today, I find it difficult to consider the work with Quality Circles a success. The intention was to involve our employees—the practical results for the company were rather limited compared to all the efforts which were put into the Circles. The reasons for the rather negative results are probably several. The Circles selected their tasks themselves. This means there was no link between the work of most of the Circles and high priority issues of the company. . . . Middle management felt that unreasonably large resources were wasted on unimportant tasks . . . [and] gave low or no priority to the follow-up of recommendations from the Circles. This in turn led to frustration among many of the members."

Once the necessary training and support are available, employee participation in performance improvement through quality should progressively manifest itself through:

1. Training in quality concepts and tools.

2. Providing suggestions.

3. Participating on departmental process teams (QCs).

4. Participating on cross-departmental teams.

5. Participating on self-directed and self-managed teams.

6. Leading and facilitating teams.

Customer–Supplier Partnerships

A favorite example of the difference in results obtained from treating suppliers as adversaries, versus treating them like partners, comes from the automotive industry. During an American automobile manufacturer's benchmarking visit to a Japanese automobile manufacturer's plant, they discovered that they shared a common supplier. When the American manufacturer began to disparage the supplier, his Japanese counterpart was visibly surprised. In fact, the common supplier was rated as one of the best at the Japanese plant. The major difference discovered was that the Japanese manufacturer shared early product and process design plans with the supplier. The American manufacturer did not. Through obtaining early design information, the supplier had made valuable suggestions on product design, part selection, and the manufacturing process in which the vendor's parts were to be used. Godfrey (1992) cited another example of the advantages of working in partnership with suppliers. "A recent study of the automotive industry provided a striking result. The researchers compared three auto assembly plants: one Japanese in Japan, one Japanese in North America, and one American in North America. The inventory cycle time for the American-owned plant was two weeks. The Japanese plant in America was achieving a two-day cycle time. The Japanese plant in Japan was running at a two-hour cycle time."

Quality System

In the fourth edition of *Juran's Quality Control Handbook* (1988), the term quality function is defined as "the entire collection of activities through which we achieve fitness for use, no matter where those activities are performed." Peach (1994), referencing

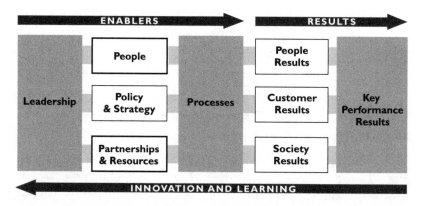

Figure 1.8   The European Quality Award Criteria: Systems View.

ISO 8402 (1994), *Quality Management and Quality Assurance—Vocabulary,** provides a similar definition for the term quality system: "the organizational structure, responsibilities, procedures, processes and resources needed to implement quality management." In the context of the previous material, a quality system encompasses the concepts, processes, and tools required to implement, review, and improve the model for managing quality. The most comprehensive tools for assessing the scope and efficacy of quality systems are the Baldrige criteria and their international counterparts (e.g., the European Quality Award).† Figure 1.8 is the European Quality Award System's perspective; model analogue to the Baldrige criteria system model (Figure 1.2).

Previous chapter materials have discussed the more limited quality system perspective provided by the ISO 9000 standards. Additional justification for recognizing the current limitations of the ISO standards is provided by Peach (1994): "ISO 9001, ISO

---

* International Organization for Standardization publications may be located and ordered from the WEB address: http://www.iso.ch/welcome.html.
† The European Quality Award is administered by the European Foundation for Quality Management (EFQM) in Brussels, Belgium. Additional information may be obtained from the WEB site: http://www.efqm.org.

9002, and ISO 9003 requirements do not constitute a full-fledged total quality management system; rather, they provide *many* of the basic building blocks for such a system."

OPERATIONAL PROCESSES FOR MANAGING QUALITY

Juran (1985, 1989) has defined three *operational* processes for managing quality: (1) *Quality Planning*, (2) *Quality Control*, and (3) *Quality Improvement*. Together they comprise the Juran Trilogy of processes required to manage for quality in operations (Figure 1.9).

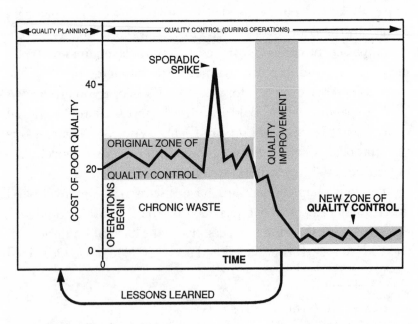

Figure 1.9 The Juran Trilogy.

From the previous perspective of the two dimensions of quality—features and deficiencies—the Quality Planning process is focused on developing product, process, and quality control *characteristics/features* that will result in meeting external and internal customers' needs. The Quality Control process is focused on minimizing the frequency of occurrence and duration of sporadic deficiencies in process and products, and the Quality Improvement process is focused on discovering the cause(s) of chronic deficiencies that result in customer dissatisfaction, protracted cycle times, and unnecessary costs. Once the type of project is identified, an appropriate process can be used to complete it. Table 1.4 provides the major steps comprising each of the processes in Juran's Trilogy.

Table 1.4 Universal Processes for Managing Quality

Quality Planning	Quality Control	Quality Improvement
Establish quality goals.	Choose control subjects.	Prove the need.
Identify customers.	Choose units of measure.	Identify projects.
Discover customer needs.	Set goals.	Organize project teams.
Develop product features.	Create a sensor.	Diagnose the causes.
Develop process features.	Measure actual performance.	Provide remedies, prove that the remedies are effective.
Establish process controls, transfer to operations.	Interpret the difference.	Deal with resistance to change.
	Take action on the difference.	Control to hold the gains.

Source: Juran and Gryna (1993).

Examples of Quality Planning projects include the design of a new Automated Voice Response System by Zeidler (1993) at Florida Power & Light Company, redesigning a Quality Information System by Jennison and Jordon (1991) at Harvard Community Health Plan, and redesigning Computer-Aided Engineering systems at Delval-Stork in the Netherlands by Scherp (1994). Examples of Quality Control projects include controlling response times to questions from field personnel collecting data for the Consumer Price Index at the Bureau of Labor Statistics (Dmytrow, 1985); controlling the quality of input data for service orders at AT&T (Hue, Pautke, & Redman, 1992); and controlling the mailing dates for the Vanguard Group's clients'

Figure 1.10 Juran Institute's Model for Managing Quality (Detailed View).

statements (Wright, 1995). Examples of Quality Improvement projects range from reducing chronic levels of solder defects by 62 percent, as reported by Betker at GTE (1983), to reducing the length of stay for carotid endarterectomies by 44 percent, reported by Bartelson (1996) at the Mayo Foundation. Additional examples of the application of the Trilogy are provided in subsequent chapters.

Integrating the Modules for Results

As each of the macrolevel modules for managing quality is implemented, the modules combine to produce the detailed model and results shown in Figure 1.10 on page 24.

Comparisons with Other Organizational Performance Assessment Models

Table 1.5 on pages 26–27 provides a basis for cross-linking the Juran Institute model's components with the categories and elements of the Baldrige, Deming, and European Quality Award performance model criteria (1993).

The Need for a Road Map

Once the model for managing quality is understood and endorsed by upper management, an implementation plan is needed. A road map for developing and executing an implementation

Table 1.5 Relationships of Juran Total Quality Management Model to Selected Quality System Assessment Criteria

Juran Institute TQM Element	U.S. Baldrige National Quality Award Categories	Japan Deming Prize Checklist Categories	European Quality Award Categories
Delighted customers	7.0 Customer Focus & Satisfaction	9. Results	6. Customer Satisfaction
Empowered employees	4.2 Employee Involvement 4.5 Employee Well-Being and Satisfaction	2(2) Delegation of Authority 2(6) Utilization of QC Circles 3(6) QC Circle Activities 3(7) Suggestion System	3d How to Promote Involvement 7. People Satisfaction
Higher revenue	(Implicit)	9(2) Substantive Results	9. Business Results
Lower cost	6.0 Quality & Operational Results	9(2) Substantive Results	4a Financial Resources 9. Business Results
Quality control	5.2a How to Maintain Quality of Product & Service 5.3a How to Maintain Quality of Business & Support Service Processes	7. Control	5a,b How to Manage Key Processes
Quality planning	7.1 Customer Expectations: Current & Future 5.1 Design & Introduction of Quality Products & Services 5.3a How Business & Support Services Processes Are Designed	8(1) Procedcure for New Product Development Standardization 8(3) Process Design 8(4) Process Capability 5(5) Quality Analysis 6. Standardization	(Implicit in 6. Customer Satisfaction)

Quality improvement	5.2b How to Improve Quality of Product & Service 5.3b How to Improve Quality of Business Process & Support	5. Analysis	5c-e Process Improvement
Quality system	5.0 Management of Process Quality	8. Quality Assurance	5. Processes
Customer-supplier partnerships	5.4 Supplier Quality 6.4 Supplier Quality Results 7.2 Customer Relationship Management	8(7) Vendor Control	1c Recognition, Including Suppliers
Total organization involvement	4.0 Human Resource Development Management	2. Organization and Its Management	3. People Management
Measurement & information	2.0 Information & Analysis	4. Collection, Dissemination & Use of Information	4b Information Resources
Education & training	4.3 Employee Education & Training	3 Education & Its Dissemination	3b How to Preserve and Develope Core Skills
Strategic quality management	3.0 Strategic Quality Planning	10. Planning for the Future 1. Policy	2. Policy & Strategy
Executive leadership	1.0 Leadership	1. Policy	1. Leadership
Customer focus	7.0 Customer Focus & Satisfaction	1. Policy	6. Customer Satisfaction 8. Impact on Society

plan is introduced in Chapter 2. The overview will define and explain the phases of a *typical* implementation plan. Subsequent chapters provide examples of how organizations actually progressed through the phases of implementing the road map, the results they achieved, and the lessons they learned.

HIGHLIGHTS OF CHAPTER 1

1. A key determinant of an organization's long-term viability is its rate of improvement versus its competition (including, for government entities, privatization). Accelerated performance improvement can be accomplished through managing for quality.

2. Partial responses, including reengineering and ISO 9000, have produced limited results.

3. The Baldrige and European Quality criteria have facilitated understanding of the need to manage performance from the systems view.

4. Achieving revolutionary results requires that quality goals be integrated throughout organizations' strategic and operational processes.

5. The two major dimensions of quality are *features* and *deficiencies:*

   a. Features produce customer satisfaction and increase market share.

   b. Deficiencies yield customer dissatisfaction and increase costs.

6. Juran Institute's model for managing quality has been used to design and implement the infrastructure required to manage the two dimensions of quality throughout all types of organizations.

7. A road map for developing and executing an implementation plan for the model is presented in Chapter 2.

References

Ambrose, B. (1992). "Short's Total Quality Programme Making Champions Out of Skeptics," *Proceedings Juran Institute's European Quality Conference,* Juran Institute, Wilton, CT.

Ambrose, B. (1990). "Short's Company-Wide Quality Improvement Program," *Proceedings Juran Institute's IMPRO Conference,* Juran Institute, Wilton, CT.

Andreas, O.A. (1992). "Quality Management I Det Norske Veritas—Experiences from the 80's and Expectations for the 90's," *Proceedings Juran Institute's EUROQUAL Conference,* Juran Institute, Wilton, CT.

Bartelson, J.D. (1996). "Major Results Quickly," *Proceedings Juran Institute's Conference on Managing for Total Quality,* Juran Institute, Wilton, CT.

Betker, H.A. (1983). "Reducing Solder Defects on Printed Circuit Board Assemblies," *Proceedings Juran Institute's IMPRO Conference,* Juran Institute, Wilton, CT.

Bradshaw, K. (August 9, 1998). "Analysis: Big Changes at G.M." *New York Times.*

Coletti, J.O. (1994). "Alive And Kicking . . . The Tradition Continues," *Proceedings of Symposium on Management for Quality in Research and Development,* Juran Institute, Wilton, CT.

Cornish, H.T. (1988). "Can Juran Solve All Our Quality Problems?" *Proceedings Juran Institute's IMPRO Conference,* Juran Institute, Wilton, CT.

Dmytrow, E.D. (1985). "Process Capability in the Service Sector," *The Juran Report,* No. 5, Juran Institute, Wilton, CT.

Endres, A.C. (1997). *Improving R&D Performance The Juran Way,* John Wiley & Sons, New York, NY.

Fuchs, E., and Wyndrum, R.W. (1995). "The Role of Leaders in TQM Transformations," *Proceedings Juran Institute's Conference on Managing for Total Quality,* Juran Institute, Wilton, CT.

Godfrey, A.B. (1992). "World-Class Quality: Some Thoughts on Obvious Trends in the 1990s," *Proceedings Juran Institute's EUROQUAL Conference*, Juran Institute, Wilton, CT.

Harry, M. (May, 1998). "Six Sigma: A Breakthrough Strategy for Profitability," *Quality Progress*, Milwaukee, WI.

Hue, Y.U., Pautke, R.W., and Redman, T.C. (1992). "Data Quality Control," *Proceedings, International Software Quality Exchange*, Juran Institute, Wilton, CT.

ISO 8402. (1994). *Quality Management and Quality Assurance—Vocabulary*, International Organization for Standardization, Geneva, Switzerland.

Jennison, K., and Jordon, H. (1991). "A Quality Information System for Health Care TQM," *Proceedings Juran Institute's IMPRO Conference*, Juran Institute, Wilton, CT.

Juran, J.M. (1995). *A History of Managing for Quality*, ASQC Quality Press, Milwaukee, WI.

Juran, J.M. (1993). "Made in U.S.A.: A Renaissance in Quality," *Harvard Business Review*, July–August, Harvard Business School, Boston, MA.

Juran, J.M. (1992). *Juran on Quality by Design*, Free Press, New York, NY.

Juran, J.M. (1990). "Made in USA: A Break in the Clouds," Quest for Excellence conference, Washington, DC.

Juran, J.M. (1989). *Juran on Leadership for Quality*, Free Press, New York, NY.

Juran, J.M. (1988). *Juran's Quality Control Handbook* (4th Edition), McGraw-Hill, New York, NY.

Juran, J.M. (1985). "IMPRO 85 Closing Remarks," *Proceedings Juran Institute's IMPRO Conference*, Juran Institute, Wilton, CT.

Juran, J.M. (1981). "Product Quality—A Prescription for the West," 25th Conference, European Organization for Quality Control, Paris, France.

Juran, J.M., and Gryna, F.M. (1993). *Quality Planning and Analysis* (3rd Edition), McGraw-Hill, New York, NY.

Leak, M.C. (1988). "Quality Education as a Management System," *Proceedings Juran Institute's IMPRO Conference*, Juran Institute, Wilton, CT.

Leo, R.J. (1994). "A Corporate Business Excellence Process," *Proceedings Juran Institute's Conference on Managing for Total Quality*, Juran Institute, Wilton, CT.

Main, J. (1994). *Quality Wars*, Free Press, New York, NY.

Murphy, J.R. (1988). "Process Is Not Strategy—Training Managers and Employees to Carry Out a Strategy-Based Quality Plan," *Proceedings Juran Institute's IMPRO Conference*, Juran Institute, Wilton, CT.

National Institute of Standards and Technology Website. (1999). "NIST Stock Study Shows Quality Pays," http://www.quality.nist.gov /nqpwsmap.htm.

National Institute of Standards and Technology, *1999 Criteria for Performance Excellence*, National Quality Program, Gaithersburg, MD.

Norton, D.P. (1997). "Using the Balanced Scorecard: Measures That Drive Performance," Handout from PBS Satellite Service Videoconference, sponsored by the University of Tampa's Center for Quality, Tampa, FL.

Palermo, R.C., and Watson, G.H. (1993). *A World of Quality*, ASQC Press, Milwaukee, WI.

Peach, R.W. (1994). *The ISO 9000 Handbook*, (2nd Edition), CEEM Information Services, Fairfax, VA.

Reiman, C.W., and Hertz, H.S. (1993). "The Malcolm Baldrige National Quality Award and ISO 9000 Registration: Understanding Their Many Differences," National Institute of Standards and Technology, Gaithersburg, MD.

Rocca, C.J. (1991). "Rochester Excellence . . . Customer Satisfaction . . . The Journey Continues," *Proceedings of Symposium on Management for Quality in Research and Development*, Juran Institute, Wilton, CT.

Sandholm, L. (1992). "Training in Quality—From Board Room to Shop Floor," *Proceedings Juran Institute's EUROQUAL Conference*, Juran Institute, Wilton, CT.

Scherp, O.P. (1994). "Using Quality Planning to Implement Computer-Aided Engineering," *Proceedings Juran Institute's Conference on Managing for Total Quality*, Juran Institute, Wilton, CT.

Waller, R.R. (1996). "The Best of Both Worlds: Better Care and Lower Costs," *Proceedings Juran Institute's Conference on Managing for Total Quality*, Juran Institute, Wilton, CT.

Welch, J., Dammerman, D.D., Murphy, E.F., and Opie, J.D. (1998). *General Electric Company 1998 Annual Report*, Fairfield, CT.

Whitaker, A.L. (1995). "People—The Key to Global Competitiveness," *Proceedings Juran Institute's Conference on Managing for Total Quality*, Juran Institute, Wilton, CT.

Wright, C.E. (1995). "Statement Efficiency Improvement Process," *Proceedings Juran Institute's IMPRO Conference*, Juran Institute, Wilton, CT.

Zachman, J.W. (1990). "Developing and Executing Business Strategies Using Process Quality Management," *Proceedings Juran Institute's IMPRO Conference*, Juran Institute, Wilton, CT.

Zeidler, P.C. (1993). "Using Quality Function Deployment to Design and Implement a Voice Response Unit at Florida Power & Light Company," *Proceedings of Symposium on Managing for Quality in Research and Development*, Juran Institute, Wilton, CT.

CHAPTER 2

A Road Map for Accelerating Performance

Introduction

The previous chapter presented a model in which the components provide the necessary framework for leading and managing quality. The purpose of the model is to identify the necessary *concepts and processes* required to accelerate organizations' performance through quality. Quality was presented as an exemplary means for enhancing performance through simultaneously reducing costs and cycle times, while concomitantly increasing customer satisfaction, employee satisfaction, and market share. This chapter will introduce a road map (Juran Institute, 1995) that, when followed, will result in the actual development of the concepts and processes comprising the model. Additional insights are provided via examples of several organizations' drivers and approaches for planning and implementing their quality initiatives.

On Juran's Road to Total Quality Management

Figure 2.1 presents a macrolevel view of the multiphased journey to implementing a Total Quality Management (TQM) process. In the context of the previous chapter, the journey should be viewed only as a means for enabling an organization to drive performance improvement through empowered employees whose goals and actions are aligned with the organization's strategy for delighting customers with world-class products provided at minimum costs.

The purpose and general objectives of each of the *phases* of the quality journey—*Decide, Prepare, Start, Expand, and Integrate*—

Figure 2.1 The Road to TQM and Performance Improvement.

are defined in separate sections. Details and examples relevant to the Decide Phase are also provided. Subsequent chapters discuss details and examples of successfully designing and implementing each of the remaining phases. Checklists of actions recommended for senior managers are provided for each of the phases.

The Decide Phase

The general purpose of the *Decide Phase* is to gain these informed commitments from senior management:

1. We understand and are prepared to communicate the reasons/drivers for embarking on a quality journey.

2. Relative to our current culture, we understand and accept the *basic* premises and concepts required for Total Quality Management versus other partial approaches.

3. We understand the type and magnitude of resources that will be required to successfully complete the quality journey, and we are willing to provide them.

The Prepare Phase

When the senior managers make an informed decision to initiate their organization's quality initiative, they must prepare themselves and the rest of the organization for their journey. Chapter 3 provides and discusses the recommended "shopping list" of activities to prepare for the journey. Key types of activities within the *Prepare Phase* include *organizing, staffing, training* (beyond basic concepts), and *communicating* (to everyone) the need for the journey, the goals, the plan for accomplishing the goals, and how to measure progress against the plan.

The Start Phase

When the organization has prepared to begin its quality journey, it enters the *Start Phase*. The primary objectives for the Start Phase are:

1. Successfully complete relevant pilot projects (identified during the Prepare Phase), and demonstrate that the organization's quality initiative is capable of quickly producing significant results that benefit both the organization's employees and its customers.

2. Review the lessons learned from the pilot projects to identify and build from the best practices, and improve the rest.

3. Design, develop, and implement an infrastructure of key processes (e.g., for project nominations, facilitator and team training, reward and recognition) that is needed to expand the quality initiative throughout the organization.

The Expand Phase

The purpose of the *Expand Phase* is to multiply the benefits from the Start Phase. The enhancements are accrued through utilizing the infrastructure elements developed in the Start Phase to:

1. Increase the *scope of the organizational infrastructure* (e.g., organize quality councils at different divisions or operations centers).

2. Increase the *number of projects.*

3. Increase the *types of projects* (e.g., instead of focusing primarily on Quality Improvement, include Quality Planning and Quality Control projects).

4. Expand the *type of training* for facilitators and teams to support each type of project.

5. Enhance and align the quality assessment and measurement system to provide the information for planning, leading, and managing quality throughout the organization.

The Integrate Phase

The terms *TQM, Reengineering,* and *Empowerment* may rise and fall in popularity. Irrespective of the name, what is important is the benefits that they do or do not produce. A key to the successful expansion and perpetuation of significant results is to integrate the processes producing the results into the way the organization "does business." Experience suggests that the benefits are most likely to be gained (and sustained) when the approaches are "grafted" to the "accepted" business processes, such as strategic planning, reviewing progress, and rewarding results. Therefore, the primary objective for the *Integrate Phase* is to successfully "graft" the concepts, processes, and tools of TQM onto the ongoing strategic and operational business practices.

Detailing the Decide Phase

Figure 2.2 provides a detailed view of the TQM road map's Decide Phase. Many facets of the Decide Phase have been discussed in Chapter 1. However, Figure 2.2 offers a useful summary view of the *Drivers* for accelerating performance improvements. For example, at Duracell, C. Robert Kidder (Chairman and Chief Executive Officer) stated that:

> The rationale to embark on a TQM initiative was based on several key factors:
>
> • Growing concern about product quality.
>
> • Growing concern about product consistency.
>
> • Competitive threat, especially from Japan.

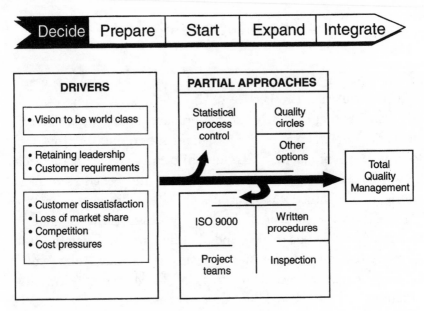

Figure 2.2 Decide Phase: Drivers and Detours.

- Pressure from OEMs.
- Sourcing alkaline because of quality.
- Lithium recall.
- Reducing levels of scrap.
- Monitoring customer service performance.
- Cultural issues (teamwork, cooperation).
- TQM was working at other companies. (Kidder, Kiernan, and Correll, 1993).

Too many organizations have become detoured during their quality journeys because they became enamored with one or more of the *Partial Approaches* listed in Figure 2.2. Table 2.1 provides a checklist of deeds to be done by an organization's upper managers when they seek to successfully complete the Decide Phase.

Assessing Quality Status

A key responsibility of any organization's leaders is to conduct periodic broad assessments of the organization's *overall* performance.

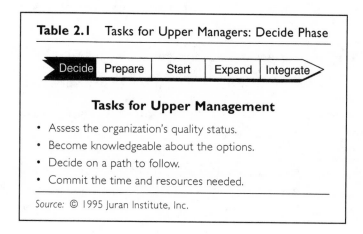

Table 2.1   Tasks for Upper Managers: Decide Phase

Decide	Prepare	Start	Expand	Integrate

Tasks for Upper Management

- Assess the organization's quality status.
- Become knowledgeable about the options.
- Decide on a path to follow.
- Commit the time and resources needed.

Source: © 1995 Juran Institute, Inc.

Traditional names of these assessment processes have included Strengths, Weaknesses, Opportunities, Threats (SWOT) reviews, and Situational Analyses. Completion of these reviews provides an organization's leaders with the information needed to review its progress in defining and implementing its strategy within the context of its values. These reviews should result in an informed decision to do one of the following:

1. Continue with its current strategy.

2. Change its strategy.

3. Change its current vision and mission, redefine its critical success factors (CSFs), and develop new strategies for the new CSFs.

A key *dimension* of any assessment should provide answers to questions such as: Relative to current or anticipated competition, where are we in terms of the quality (features and deficiencies) of the goods or services we provide to our key customers? The answer will correspondingly provide the information required for "Proof of the Need" to do one of the following:

1. Focus on maintaining the organization's current quality status (and rate of progress).

2. Refine its current strategy for managing quality.

3. Redesign its current strategy for managing quality.

4. Prepare to start developing a systems approach to managing for quality.

At Caterpillar, Black (1989) provided an early example of Caterpillar's perception of the drivers for leading and managing quality, Caterpillar's responses, and its results:

In the dark days of 1982, Caterpillar sought a new approach to quality strategy, We were, without question, under fire. After 50 years of uninterrupted growth, we found ourselves facing unprecedented worldwide competition. Previously, our competitors had mostly been U.S.-based exporters like ourselves. Those U.S. competitors had cost bases similar to our own, and because of superior engineering and product support experience, we found them relatively easy to compete with. But our new non-U.S. competitors had radically lower cost bases. They used this factor to create a price gap—exacerbated by the overvalued U.S. dollar—to get customers to try them out. Unfortunately, many of those customers were impressed with the value these non-U.S. manufacturers, mostly Japanese, offered. Once competitors established toeholds, they used a powerful technique to move "higher"—in value-added terms—in the market. This technique, new to us at the time, was making continuous quality improvements at rates we had never before faced.

We'd been making quality improvements all along, of course. After all, we were and are recognized as the quality leaders in our industry. But we hadn't approached quality improvement with the same relentless, disciplined commitment that some of our competitors had. The gap was closing. When those non-U.S. competitors began to take some of our customers, we learned a lesson. It was absolutely imperative that we find a path to greater competitiveness by the year 2000. It would require accelerated quality improvement. Without it, we'd end up like much of our former U.S. competition—extinct.

Our response to this crisis took several forms. One action was to research the ideas of the most prominent quality practitioners. And as a result, we invited Dr. Juran to meet with our company officers in 1982. Dr. Juran's thinking had immediate appeal within the Caterpillar culture. Our officers— and soon, many others throughout our organization—became acquainted with such familiar concepts as the Juran Trilogy, breakthrough sequence, project-by-project methodology, and so forth.

Many of you in this audience have had similar experiences. And I suspect that many of you have also found that solid results are the only antidote to that resistance. In our case, if Dr. Juran had given us his 16 videos at no charge and had asked for just a 5 percent share of the benefits, he would now be the recipient of a tidy fortune. More than 2,500 Caterpillar AQI teams have completed or are in the process of completing projects; our accumulated savings total at least $327 million so far. And we know we haven't been able to account for all savings.

Caterpillar's equipment is used both domestically and internationally by the construction industry. Moron and Ledbetter (1992) have provided insights into the Dragados Y Construcciones perspective and their plan to embark on their TQM journey (note that a key issue, raised early, is the decision on *whether* and *how* to utilize a TQM consultant):

Spain is a rapidly expanding, highly developed country poised for full partnership in the European Economic Community (EEC). Competition will be intense as this unprecedented historical event occurs. One major company, Dragados Group, is dedicated toward springing from a position of excellence in Spain to becoming one of the leading companies throughout the EEC. Dragados Group is a large company with around $4 billion in volume annually. Their primary focus is construction (highways, bridges, tunnels, toll roads, dams, energy, industrial, and the like, mainly within Spain). They have in-house design and construction capabilities, with several other business thrusts supporting design and construction. With over 16,000 employees working throughout the world, they have a sophisticated, project-based organization.

To continue to grow and prosper, Dragados decided to embark on a journey toward TQM. Following are the steps they have taken thus far on that journey:

Step 1. Realize the Problem and DECIDE. Dragados examined the construction industry in the forthcoming EEC, the Far East, and the United States, and concluded they had a problem. To remain competitive, they had to become more cost-effective. To continue to grow and prosper in the new environment, they had to take a quantum leap forward through a step-change in the way they conducted business. The success of TQM in Japan and the U.S. convinced Dragados that TQM was the way to go. The result of step 1 was a commitment at the top for embarking on TQM. This was vital. Without it, the effort will fail!

Step 2. Select a Consultant. Dragados recognized that they would not succeed if they embarked on this journey without expert help. The three alternatives they considered were (1) select a few Dragados managers and send them to public TQM training courses and then have them direct the effort within Dragados; (2) select a consultant to train selected personnel within Dragados and then leave; or (3) select a consultant to work with the firm on a longer-term basis to provide training and to assist Dragados during the early stages in establishing the TQM management system required to fully implement TQM. The third alternative was selected for several reasons. First, the consultant brought legitimacy and expertise, which would result in a higher probability of Dragados embracing this new approach. Second, while the Dragados managers could be rapidly trained in the basics, they could not become experts for a lengthy period, during which time Dragados would be experiencing many false starts, wasteful expenditures, and relatively slow progress. A short-term consultant would not help Dragados avoid pitfalls down the road. The longer-term consultant would speed up the process, help Dragados avoid the many roadblocks, and reduce the total cost of implementing a TQM program.

Once the decision was made on hiring a consultant, the next question was "Which one?" As the construction industry is unique, a consultant knowledgeable in developing TQM programs in construction industry companies was needed. The result was a TQM Implementation Partnership (TIP) between the Juran Institute (a world leader in TQM implementation) and W.B. Ledbetter (an expert in TQM related to the construction industry). The TQM Implementation Partnership (TIP) committed to assist Dragados long enough to ensure Dragados self-sufficiency in implementing TQM. . . .

Shifting from examples of the Decide Phase in the international construction industry to financial services, John Brennan (1991), reporting as President of The Vanguard Group of Investment companies, discussed Vanguard's reasons for deciding to start their TQM journey:

We are confident of the need for programs like TQM to keep us on the leading edge of high quality standards. Why? First, there is the old adage, which states, "Treat your customers like they own your business." Few companies actually follow this advice. But at Vanguard we are compelled to do so as our customers in fact do own the company! We have no stockholders per se, which means that the success we achieve is shared only with those investors who choose to entrust their hard-earned financial resources with our Crew members. For both these constituencies—our clients and our Crew—our success translates into growing financial independence for individuals and their families. Is there a mission aside from health and happiness that is more vital?

Second, Vanguard is a rapidly expanding organization. Our precipitate growth reflects a high level of confidence in Vanguard's performance; however, it also represents a significant challenge—the challenge to shoulder the ever-increasing responsibility our growth has wrought, while continuing to improve our service and retain the characteristics that have made us a leader in our industry.

Finally, there is the not insignificant danger of complacency. Our record of growth is indeed an enviable one. But we accept the message of caution that we so frequently pass along to our shareholders: Past success is no guarantee of future success. Herein lies another vital—perhaps the greatest—challenge for Vanguard, one which we recognize, accept, and plan to meet through our pursuit of Total Quality Management.

A final comprehensive example of the use of assessment to set the context for Kaiser Permanente's Ohio Region's quality strategy and initiative has been provided by Bolmey et al. (1992):

In 1988, the senior management of the region began a systematic and comprehensive assessment of the rapidly changing marketplace and of our internal capacity to respond to the challenge posed by a volatile health care environment. The goal of this assessment was to formulate the strategic direction for the region: A strategy that was intended to take us through the decade of the nineties and beyond. The assessment process utilized study teams or task forces that were assisted by internal staff and outside consultants. Learning from the experiences of other organizations, both within and outside of health care, was an important part of the process.

The final assessment was achieved through a process that engaged our key managers regionwide in various discussion and focus groups. In addition, customer input was a critical component used in the assessment. The assessment process led to the identification of three major challenges or vulnerabilities facing the organization:

• The need to continuously improve the value of the service that we provide our customers and the need to demonstrate that value to all customers.

- The need to continuously attract and retain the highest-quality and best-prepared employees and providers of care in all facets of a broad-based health care organization.

- The need to have an organizational structure which places the customer at the center, and which provides the appropriate accountabilities and incentives to meet the needs of all customers.

The assessment also concluded that we needed a clear and written vision for the organization. A set of statements that would provide the region with a road map for the future. A vision that would provide a picture of the type of organization we were, and in some cases, the type of organization we sought to become. The vision, and a subsequent value statement, provided what turned out to be an important foundation for our Total Quality Management effort. These documents provided a context of Total Quality Management as a key strategic requirement. It defined Total Quality Management as a management concept and a set of tools that would help us reach our desired state.

Knowledge

Once it is *decided* that quality is to become an element of an organization's strategy, senior managers are very well advised to become knowledgeable about the *primary* differences among available paths (strategies) for managing quality. In *Juran on Quality Leadership*, Juran (1988) concluded that one of the primary reasons for the failure of so many quality initiatives is that the senior managers chose the wrong strategy for implementing quality. They chose the wrong strategy because they were not educated in the basics of available concepts and approaches for managing quality. Bolmey et al. (1992) provided additional guidance for how to determine which path to follow:

> The process described above not only provided a context for Total Quality Management but also resulted in a clear commitment from our top regional management. Similar to other organizations at this juncture, the question became, "Just how do we move forward to achieve this commitment?" Typical of our culture, a multidisciplinary task force once again was chartered to address implementation. Specifically, the task force's charge was:
>
> • To learn about Total Quality Management.
> • To learn how other organizations have successfully transitioned into Total Quality Management.
> • To develop an implementation blueprint for our organization.

Committing Resources

Table 1.3 provided a checklist for upper managers. A key requirement was the provision of the necessary resources for successfully designing and implementing their organization's chosen quality strategy. Providing the resources (and rewards) also sends a clear message to the organization: "This is not just another program!" For example, at the Vanguard Group, Berry (1991) has reported that a key responsibility of Vanguard's senior managers is to approve the financial and human resources required to implement and administer the TQM process. Another resource that can confirm this message is the *time* to plan, develop, and implement the infrastructure, as discussed in Chapter 1. Juran (1990) has also discussed the resources and infrastructure required to achieve dramatic breakthroughs in results:

> Those achieved results did not come free—they were a return on resources. A major category of those resources provided the infrastructure without which there would be few quality improvements. Let me note here that to make improvements by the thousands requires quite an organized effort—an infrastructure. A process is needed for choosing the projects to be tackled. Teams must be organized and assigned to carry out the projects. The teams must be provided with a well-designed process for making improvements. The teams need to be trained in how to operate as teams, as well as in how to diagnose problems and provide remedies. Each improvement project requires multiple team meetings, and much homework between meetings. A review process is needed to monitor progress and to help teams which get stuck. Collectively it is a lot of work, and it requires corresponding resources.

A Checklist for Upper Managers: Decide Phase

Before entering the Prepare Phase, the senior management team is well advised to review and objectively answer the following questions:

1. Do we understand and are we prepared to communicate the reasons/drivers for embarking on a quality journey? (Yes, No)

2. Relative to our current culture, do we understand the *basic* advantages and challenges to implementing Total Quality Management versus other (partial) approaches? (Yes, No)

3. Are we willing to learn, practice, and apply the knowledge and skills we need to lead a successful quality revolution? (Yes, No)

4. Do we understand the type and magnitude of resources that will be required to successfully complete our quality journey, and are we willing to provide them? (Yes, No)

One or more negative responses should be interpreted as an early warning sign: Dangerous Road Ahead!

HIGHLIGHTS OF CHAPTER 2

1. Based on experience with hundreds of companies, the model for managing quality discussed in Chapter 1 is best developed by following a road map.

2. The road map defines a journey consisting of five phases: *Decide, Prepare, Start, Expand,* and *Integrate.*

3. The rationale for dividing the journey into the five phases is to help ensure, respectively, that:

   a. The reasons (in terms of the organization's status and strategy) for the journey are understood and accepted by the senior managers.

   b. That early planning is done to prepare for a successful journey by avoiding detours.

   c. Before premature standardization and expansion, the lessons learned from early projects are reviewed and acted on.

d. The number and types of projects, and the measures used, are expanded throughout the organization.

e. The model's infrastructure has been developed and becomes the way of doing business.

References

Berry, T.H. (1991). *Managing the Total Quality Transformation*, ASQC Quality Press, Milwaukee, WI.

Black, S.P. (1989). "AQI 2000," *Proceedings Juran Institute's IMPRO Conference*, Juran Institute, Wilton, CT.

Bolmey, A., McNab, P., and Yuhasz, N. (1992). "Kaiser Permanente—The Implementation of Total Quality Management in a Large, Decentralized Health Care Organization," *Proceedings Juran Institute's IMPRO Conference*, Juran Institute, Wilton, CT.

Brennan, J.J. (1991). "Investing in Quality at the Vanguard Group: If It's Not Broken, Improve It Everyday Anyway," *Proceedings Juran Institute's IMPRO Conference*, Juran Institute, Wilton, CT.

Juran Institute. (1995). *The Road Toward Total Quality*, Wilton, CT.

Juran, J.M. (1990). "Made in USA: A Break in the Clouds," summary address presented at "The Quest for Excellence," an executive conference featuring the 1989 winners of the Malcolm Baldrige National Quality Award. February 22–23, 1990, Washington, DC.

Juran, J.M. (1988). *Juran on Quality Leadership*, A Videotape Produced by Juran Institute Inc., Wilton, CT.

Kidder, R., Kiernan, C., and Correll, B. (1993). "Integrating TQM to Fit Duracell's Corporate Culture," *Proceedings Juran Institute's IMPRO Conference*, Juran Institute, Wilton, CT.

Moron, J.M., and Ledbetter, W.B. (1992). "TQM Startup in a Large Construction Company," *Proceedings Juran Institute's IMPRO Conference*, Juran Institute, Wilton, CT.

CHAPTER 3

Preparing for the Journey

Introduction

When an organization has decided to undertake its quality journey, it must ensure that it is prepared for it. This chapter discusses the sequence of activities that are necessary for organizations to define, develop, and provide the resources required to start a quality journey. As in the previous chapter, there is a list of deeds for upper managers. Examples of both the activities and the supporting actions of senior managers, drawn from reports made at Juran Institute's IMPRO conferences, are provided throughout the chapter.

Defining Activities for the Prepare Phase

Figure 3.1 provides an overview of the Prepare Phase activities and their sequencing. This chapter provides details and examples for each of the activities in the Prepare Phase. After completing

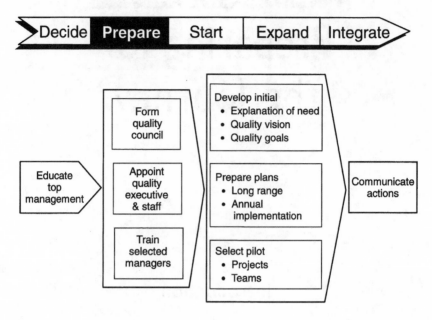

Figure 3.1 The Prepare Phase.

the Prepare Phase, the organization has established a solid basis from which its quality journey can be launched, supported, and sustained.

Educate Top Management

As a key activity of the Decide Phase, senior managers gained a broad understanding of the "big picture" of the quality status of their organization, and the strategies available for managing quality. Then, armed with an understanding of the magnitude of their organizations' quality "opportunities" and a general under-standing of the various approaches, they could make an *informed* decision on the strategy/path they wanted to follow to accelerate performance improvement. During the Prepare Phase, senior managers must *enhance* their knowledge of the chosen strategy in sufficient detail to help their organizations plan and initiate the activities required for their quality journeys.

The required knowledge is typically gained from participating in one or more workshops focused on defining, developing, implementing, and communicating:

1. The initial infrastructure required to support the quality journey.

2. An implementation plan for guiding and checking progress.

3. Selection and support of appropriate pilot projects.

An early example of the type and extent of the training needed for senior managers was defined by Wesley Howe (1986), reporting as CEO of Beckton Dickinson:

> . . . two days of our President's Meeting were spent with Dr. Juran on the subject of quality improvement. In actual fact, our senior managers have spent three days with Dr. Juran. We were ensuring that our upper management were the first to learn the Juran concepts and techniques and were properly trained and positioned so that they could help lead the way. When we left the meeting, there was to be no doubt that all had a duty to lead our quality improvement process. We were to lead by doing. Key sessions of this meeting were videotaped for planned subsequent use at all Company locations worldwide. There could be no misunderstanding on where I and other senior managers stood on the credo, on the Juran Process, and on continual quality improvement.

Similarly, at the Aid Association for Lutherans (AAL), an organization that has over $15 billion of assets under management for its more than 1.6 million members, Gunderson (1993), reporting as President and CEO, stated:

> AAL's quality journey began officially on March 31, 1991. On that day, an executive awareness workshop was held. Attending with me were the senior executive group and a few other members of management. The purpose of the workshop was to build enthusiasm, energy, and support for Total Quality Management and share a common growth experience that would build a common understanding and vocabulary. The event also was intended to start defining quality leadership roles for top management. A significant contributor to the meeting was its leader, William A. Golomski, a person with a national reputation who had spent nearly 40 years in the quality movement. The counsel he provided made it very clear that for a quality initiative to succeed it must have both the support and the active involvement of top management. Ongoing executive participation would provide sustained leadership, create a better understanding of what was being asked of the organization, and facilitate the creation of a vision.

Form an Executive Quality Council

In addition to gaining an understanding of the concepts and vocabulary of the chosen approach, a key objective of the workshops is to drive the formation of an executive quality council. The workshop explains the role and responsibilities of the council. In fact, a useful breakout/syndicate session should be designed into the workshop, for drafting a mission statement for the council and for identifying council members. This question and statement are often heard: "Why do we need another committee and meeting? Let's just put quality on the agenda for our regular executive council meeting." A valid response would be that although the executive quality council *should* be comprised of the organization's leaders, *until the organization's leadership becomes comfortable with leading the quality journey, it is best that they at first focus on it separately.* For example, Bob Galvin (1991), the former Chairman of Motorola, found that although quality was scheduled as an agenda item, other business issues were addressed first, and there was often insufficient time left for quality. Galvin then insisted that quality be placed first on the meeting's agenda. Main (1994) states: ". . . not only did [Galvin] put quality at the top of the agenda of every meeting, but once that item of the agenda had been covered he would often leave the meeting."

Juran (1990) has proposed a list of responsibilities for Executive Quality Councils. At Beckton Dickinson, Howe (1986) provided further insights into how organizations can use quality councils to set the direction for, and to launch, their quality initiatives:

> Prior to introducing the Juran Process to 37 Company locations around the world, a Corporate-level Quality Improvement Council comprised of six Corporate Officers planned and structured the complete roll-out program. Our Chief Operating Officer chaired this Council. We knew and stated in 1983 that for our Quality Improvement Process to succeed we needed "hands-on leadership by top management." We also needed management training and participation, which started with senior Corporate and with senior division management. Our entire effort truly was top down.

Thomas Berry (1991), the Director of Quality at the Vanguard Group of Investment Companies, has worked with the author as a guest presenter at various Juran Institute workshops, and has provided the following mission and elements for the Vanguard Group's quality council:

Mission: The Vanguard Quality Council exists to carry out the corporate quality policy by directing, participating in and supporting a Total Quality Management process.

Key Responsibilities:

1. To formulate, communicate, and carry out the corporate quality policy.

2. To approve the TQM implementation plan, update it as necessary, and communicate it throughout the company.

3. To approve the financial and human resources required to implement and administer the TQM process.

4. To strategically position TQM as a high corporate priority for the long term.

5. To establish and direct the activities of senior quality steering groups in all functional areas.

6. To ensure that corporate reward and recognition systems support and reinforce TQM participation and success.

7. To monitor and communicate results achieved through the TQM process.

8. To lead the quality planning process.

9. To participate in recognition events that celebrate TQM success.

10. To ensure that adequate training is provided in TQM in order to establish an environment of continuous learning.

11. To ensure top management's personal and direct learning involvement in TQM activities, including membership on a QI team, participation in TQM training and personal contact with customers, etc.

12. To monitor the selection of quality improvement projects to ensure they are directed at key client-focused priorities and/or opportunities for internal efficiency improvements.

McCain (1995), at Kelly Services, Inc., described key responsibilities for Kelly's Quality Council:

The Quality Council developed a blueprint for determining the boundaries of its leadership and deployment role. Its most crucial responsibilities include:

- Setting and deploying Vision, Mission, Shared Values, Quality Policy, and Quality Goals.
- Reviewing progress against Quality Goals.
- Integrating Quality Goals into business plans and Performance Management.

Appoint a Quality Executive and Staff

The chief executive and his or her immediate reporting personnel have the primary responsibility for setting the *strategic direction and goals* for their organization's quality journey. However, they typically need to identify a chief quality officer who will be responsible for coordinating the development of the *operational planning* required to establish the infrastructure needed to start, expand, integrate, and report on quality throughout the organization. The Chief Financial Officer is responsible for planning and coordinating the design and implementation of the financial reporting system that is used to determine the organization's financial status, and the progress it has made in meeting its financial objectives. Correspondingly, a Chief Quality Officer is responsible for the design, development, and implementation of a quality system that provides the information on an organization's quality status.

Gunderson (1993) provided the following insights into the criteria that he used to select AAL's Chief Quality Officer (CQO):

> It would be difficult to overemphasize the importance of selecting the right people to coordinate a corporate-wide TQM initiative. Late in 1991, a Chief Quality Officer was appointed at AAL. The appointment sent another important signal to the organization about management's commitment and intentions. While several individuals were considered viable candidates, a decision was made to select a senior officer with five years of line experience for that position. In addition to a good track record of line experience, the individual selected also possessed an attractive combination of attributes and experiences that added to his effectiveness in the role of CQO, including the following:
>
> • A major participant in the planning process.
> • A consulting background.
> • Well-developed facilitation skills.
> • Excellent human relations skills.
> • Strong intellectual curiosity.
> • Deeply committed to TQM principles.
> • Committed to sharing the spotlight with others.
> • Excellent rapport with and confidence of CEO.
>
> The selection of the Chief Quality Officer was a key decision in our TQM journey. Certainly, as CEO, I need to demonstrate a leadership role for every quality effort. But, there's no substitute for an effective partnership between the CEO and the individual chosen to manage the quality effort.

At AAL, the Chief Quality Officer has served as a resource for the entire organization. He has been an important mentor to me personally. He has provided counsel and advice on many of the key issues, including what I needed to do to effectively position total quality management. Frankly, it's virtually impossible to appoint someone to manage a corporate TQM initiative who is "overqualified."

The Chief Quality Officer has been assisted by a small but highly committed and competent staff. The decision to keep the staff small has been intentional and has conveyed the message that quality is not something that is being done *to* the organization, but rather *by* the organization.

McCain (1995), at Kelly Services, provided the following "job description" for Kelly's principal quality executive and Kelly's Quality Service Department:

The Senior Vice President, Service and Quality coordinates all support for the successful design and rollout of the Kelly Quality Initiative, including communication, training, and Quality Services department [which] provides Quality-related services to Kelly organizations.

Train Selected Managers

The Quality Council and Chief Quality Officer (CQO) work together to identify key planning issues for the organization's quality journey. The development of an implementation plan is best accomplished by identifying and training key middle managers. Because middle managers typically present the greatest potential source of resistance to TQM, their participation on an implementation planning task force (typically headed by the CQO) will help identify and address their concerns. Other middle managers should be trained to help prepare their functional areas to implement the plan.

Bolmey, McNab, and Yuhasz (1992), at Kaiser Permanente, discussed the use of an implementation planning task force within Kaiser's Southern California Region:

> Similar to other organizations at this juncture, the question became, "Just how do we move forward to achieve this [Upper Management] commitment? Typical of our culture, a multidisciplinary task force once again was chartered to address implementation. Specifically, the task force's charge was:
>
> • To learn about Total Quality Management.
> • To learn how other organizations have successfully transitioned into Total Quality Management.
> • To develop an implementation blueprint for our organization.

AAL (Gunderson, 1993) prepared selected middle managers, called "divisional quality advisers" (DQAs) who:

> . . . [worked] closely with each of the senior officers. They were carefully selected and asked to commit about 20 percent of their time to TQM for 18 months. This group was given extensive quality training and has provided training to others. They have contributed significantly to the success of AAL's total quality initiative, including their leadership role on our eight initial quality improvement pilot projects.

Busch et al. (1993), at California Steel Inc. (CSI), provided the following description of the role for its continuous-improvement operational Steering Committee:

The Steering Committee provides operational support in the continuous improvement process. The Steering Committee implements the goals and strategies set forth by the Quality Council. It receives direction from and reports to the Quality Council. The Steering Committee is made up of fourteen members. The members represent middle management from throughout the company. This makes it easier to monitor TQM activity within our company by having Steering Committee members overview the process. The Steering Committee's primary responsibilities are to:

- Identify and plan training needs.
- Develop and recommend to the Quality Council nominations of Quality Improvement and Quality Planning projects.
- Implement projects selected by the Quality Council.
- Support Quality teams and Thinking Groups' activities.
- Provide for progress review of the quality process.
- Design and implement a publicity plan.
- Prepare and manage the annual TQM budget.

Select Pilot Projects and Teams

Berry (1991) and Gunderson (1993) have identified the role of the Quality Council and middle managers in selecting and supporting pilot projects. Unfortunately, many organizations have either failed to select *appropriate* pilot projects or failed to properly prepare for supporting the projects. As mentioned earlier in this chapter, in the section titled "Educate Upper Management," the senior managers should have the knowledge required to prioritize pilot projects. Correspondingly, middle managers must have the knowledge required to screen and nominate pilot projects to the Quality Council. A key issue in nominating and selecting projects is the understanding of the type of project that the team is being asked to complete. Classifying pilot projects is a crucial activity. Pilot projects have failed because untrained councils have naïvely assumed that all problems require the same solution process. This "one size fits all" blunder has led to the same training being given to all project teams—a prescription for failure. As noted in Chapter 1, Juran (1985, 1989) developed the Juran Trilogy® (see Figure 1.9, on page 22) to facilitate the classification and conduct of various types of projects.

Operational projects are classified as being associated with Quality Planning, Quality Control, or Quality Improvement opportunities.

- Quality Planning/Replanning (QP) projects arise from either:
    1. The complete *absence* of a needed product or process. An example would be the requirement for a software organization to develop its first Web-browser software package.

       or

    2. A current product/process that is so *chronically and pervasively deficient* that the only acceptable remedy is to completely replan or reengineer it. Bastian and Miller (1994), at the Los Alamos National Laboratory, reported on a QP project for replanning the process for allocating discretionary research funds.

In both cases, *either the cause of the problem is not an issue, or the cause is known to be: pervasive process inadequacies.*

- Quality Control (QC) problems are "sporadic"; they can occur during any type of process. Examples would include software "bugs" that periodically result in computer "crashes," or a bad batch of materials from a vendor that results in line stoppages. The cause(s) of the spike must be determined, to *return* the process to its *previous* level of performance. The basic question that must be answered for a Quality Control problem is: "What has *changed?*"

- Quality Improvement (QI) problems stem from processes that are *chronically* operating at unacceptable levels. In contrast to sporadic QC problems, to determine the unknown chronic causes of QI problems, the most cogent question is: "What is the underlying source(s) that have continuously led to this unacceptable level of performance?" (When the causes of the chronic deficiency level have been determined, the *remedy* may require replanning the process or product.) Here, the team's mission is to diagnose the causes and develop a remedy that will result in *"breakthroughs"* in process performance.

As stated, the process a team must follow depends on the type of project the team has been assigned (QP, QC, or QI). Juran (1985, 1989, 1992) provides and describes the relevant steps to be used for each of the Trilogy's project types. (Table 1.4, on page 23, summarizes the major steps in each of the three operational processes for managing quality.*

The purpose of pilot projects is to demonstrate significant benefits in a relatively quick time frame. Because Quality Improvement projects can be expected to produce larger returns than Quality Control projects, and are likely to be completed more quickly than Quality Planning projects, *pilot project* selection should be biased toward Quality Improvement. At Kaiser Permanente's Ohio Region, Bolmey et al. (1992) provided the following discussion on the selection of pilot projects and team members:

---

* Various "tools" have also been found useful for each type of project. For example, Zeidler (1993) describes the use of Quality Function Deployment (QFD) for planning and designing a new Voice Response Unit at Florida Power & Light Company.

First priority was to identify and select two Quality Improvement pilot projects. The selection criteria for the projects included that the project be a "winner," deal with a chronic problem area, [be] feasible, significant, [and] measurable, require multidiscipline team participation to solve, and be visible to front-line employees and have a positive impact on how they deliver service. The [Quality Council] brainstormed twenty different projects that met the pilot Quality Improvement project criteria and then used a multivoting technique to select two. Each selected project had a Region-wide scope and ramifications. Problem and Mission Statements were developed for each. (See Figure 3.2.) Team leaders and facilitators were hand-picked for each team. Since the concept of facilitators assisting the team group process was new to the Region, two facilitators per pilot project team were assigned: one physician and one nonphysician. [The Quality Council] then determined, following specific guidelines (Ailing department, Remedial, Diagnostic, etc.), which departments required representation on the teams, based on the Problem and Mission Statements. The team members were then chosen by [the council] for each department. All levels of the organization were represented on the teams, based on their knowledge of the problem to be solved. This included upper-level management, exempt and nonexempt, union and nonunion, physician and Allied Health participants. . . .

Developing Implementation Plans

The quality initiative implementation plan should clearly define:

1. The rationale for the organization's quality journey, set in the context of the organization's vision, mission, values, and supporting short and midterm goals.

1. Facilitators: Ron Hodges & Paul Schefft, M.D.
   Team Leader: Therese Sucher
   Team Members: Eddie Wills, M.D.; Coord. Urgent & Convenient Care
                   Laura Pierson; Claims & Referrals
                   Linda Bates; Customer Service
                   Martha Sigel; ISD
                   Laura Peavey, RN; Bedford Advice
                   Elinor Thomas, RN; Fairhill Urgent Care
                   Nancy Bishoff, RN; Parma Emergency Advice
                   Vera Hammond; Claims & Referrals

   Problem Statement:

   In many cases, the member and the Health Plan disagree on whether Urgent/Emergent Care should be paid by the Plan, leading to member dissatisfaction.

   Mission Statement:

   Reduce the number of cases in which there is a disagreement between Health Plan and a member on payment for Urgent/Emergent Care at a non-Plan operated facility. (Disagreements include both denials that were sustained and denials that were reversed.)

2. Facilitators: Craig George, M.D. & Chuck Seyfried
   Team Leader: Ronnie Buchman, R.N.
   Team Members: Karl Hess, M.D.; Chair - Reg. Med. Rec. Comm.
                   Barbara Rehus; ISD
                   Roy Petroff; Willoughby Medical Records
                   Kate Lloyd, RN; Clev. Hghts. Advice
                   Sandra SanFilippo, LPN; Parma Surgery
                   Kim Fitzgerald, M.D.; MLK Specialty
                   Terri Plush; Parma MOB Medical Records
                   Rich Pshock; General Srvs. - Courier Supv.

   Problem Statement:

   Consulting physicians do not have access to the ambulatory medical record for scheduled visits.

   Mission Statement:

   Increase the percentage of occurrences in which the Ambulatory Medical Record is available to the Region's internal consulting physicians for scheduled appointments.

Figure 3.2   **Kaiser Permanente Pilot Projects: Focus and Membership.**

2. Goals and detailed supporting activities and responsibilities for the first year of the journey.

3. Goals and anticipated supporting activities for the next several (two to five) years of the journey.

In 1992, Kaiser Permanente's Southern California Region reported these lessons learned in constructing its plan:

> It is imperative to develop a plan or road map of how the organization should proceed to reach its goal. However, this plan needs to be flexible to allow adaptation on the basis of the experience gained through the various phases. It is also critical to communicate the flexibility of the plan, since, in our type of organization, perception of rigidity may cause the effort to fail. Total Quality Management in a decentralized organization has to allow enough room for area differences, and recognize that there is actually more than one path to success. We have broad agreement on the principles of Total Quality Management, but at least 12 variations on the theme.
>
> A plan, regardless of how carefully it is prepared, will never anticipate all issues. Therefore, the key is to foster a learning environment—one that encourages experimentation. In other words, reality is more complex than theory, and the theory needs to be revised if appropriate. Our plan ultimately was condensed to a set of basic concepts and a handful of requirements deemed essential for success, such as: senior management direct involvement, physician involvement, need for quality councils, and training requirements.

McCain (1995), at Kelly Services, provided the implementation plan for the Kelly Quality shown in Figure 3.3.

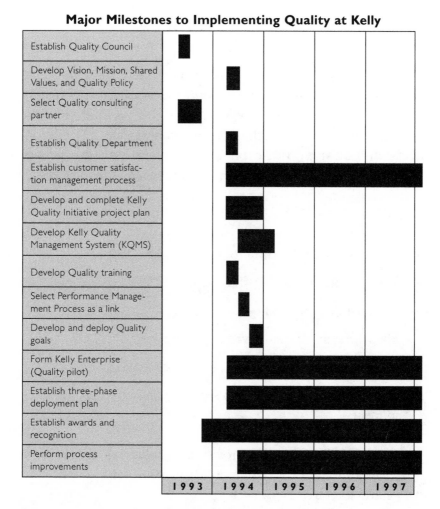

Figure 3.3 Kelly Service's TQM Implementation Plan.

Communicate Actions

Communicating an organization's reasons and plans for starting its journey promotes awareness of the organization's quality initiative and helps establish expectations. Corresponding to the real estate profession's emphasis on the importance of "Location, Location, Location," one cannot overemphasize the importance of Communicate, Communicate, Communicate. Among the specific items of information to communicate to the entire organization are:

- The reasons for deciding to start a quality initiative.
- The membership of and the role for the Quality Council.
- The goals for the quality initiative.
- The initial plans that have been completed.
- The pilot projects that have been chosen.
- The chief concerns (e.g., job security) and how they are to be addressed.

Wright (1995), at AAL, provided the following discussion of AAL's lessons learned in communicating plans for its quality initiative and its status:

> AAL has developed a fairly comprehensive plan for communicating the TQM agenda. A large part of the plan is designed to develop awareness. Awareness is measured and goals are established for achieving minimal awareness levels. The TQM Road Map is part of the promotional campaign to develop awareness of the TQM journey.

BACKGROUND

> A cross functional team of professional communicators representing each target employee audience developed the TQM communication plan.

Each quarter specific content objectives were established. For each content objective a 40% awareness goal was set. If 40% of the target audience was not aware of the intended content message, the content objective and a new approach to the communication would be attempted the next quarter. This process repeated itself until the 40% awareness goal was achieved. In most cases, the 40% awareness goal was easily achieved.

After about 2 years of following this communication approach focus groups were conducted to gain further insights into employee perception of TQM communications. Although employee awareness was high, interest in the communications was beginning to dwindle.

Four themes were repeated:

- **Hard to understand the big picture.** AAL's implementation of TQM is comprehensive. It was hard for employees to understand a single communication about an isolated TQM activity and understand how it fit into the total picture of everything going on in the TQM journey.
- **Not personally involved.** About 18% of the total employee population was personally involved in the TQM journey. It was often hard to relate to the communications.
- **Boring/over communicated.** The TQM communications were frequent, often weekly. Employees found it easy to skip over reading them, especially if not personally involved.

TQM ROAD MAP

The team identified a need to communicate in a way that illustrated the big picture of TQM at AAL and helped employees see how they contributed to and fit into that big picture.

Three communication objectives were established in an attempt to clarify the big picture:

1. Define where we have been in the TQM journey.
2. Define where we are now.
3. Define where we are going.

DEVELOPMENT PROCESS

After brainstorming several approaches the team settled on the concept of using a road map and travel themes to visually show AAL's TQM journey. Once the conceptual approach was selected, one-on-one feedback was gathered from about 25 employees. Senior executive willingness to do out-of-the-ordinary communication on quality was also verified. A prototype was developed and again tested with about 50 employees.

(Continued)

Employee focus groups were also held to review the proposed promotion plan. This input was used to modify the actual design and create the promotion plan.

A baseline measure of "big picture" awareness was taken and a follow up measure is planned. The baseline measure fell in the middle (3.4) on a 5-point scale, meaning employees are only mildly aware of where we've been, where we are and where we are going in the TQM journey.

PROMOTION

The promotional plan called for a year-long promotion anchored in the TQM Road Map. All communications on quality were to be linked back to the road map to help the reader understand how the isolated communication fit into the bigger picture. Existing communication vehicles would be used to provide updates to the journey answering the questions of where have we been, where are we or where are we going.

Periodic contests would be offered to personally involve people in a fun way in the TQM effort. A new communication vehicle, a TQM journey postcard would be reserved for highlighting results. Any new major initiatives or projects would be announced with a sticker to add to the road map. The road map would be used in TQM presentations and training whenever possible.

Plans for the initial distribution were to capitalize on the annual employee meeting. The employee meeting theme was humor in the workplace which helped give permission for this unique communication vehicle.

Along with map distribution was a contest designed like a road rally. Employees were encouraged to work in teams to complete the road rally and take their trip tic (contest form) to a main pit stop set up in the employee cafeteria. The pit stop was manned by senior executives. The pit stop area also was serving cake which encouraged those employees who had not completed the trip tic to join in the fun.

Estimates suggest over 600 of the 1700 home office employees participated in the road rally. Prizes were given to 50 randomly drawn winners in an attempt to personally involve people in the communication.

A contest involving the TQM Road Map is run every two months in the employee daily newsletter. These contests continue to address where we were, where we are and where we are going in the TQM journey.

To continue to bring the communication to the individual level, each TQM Road Map is sequentially numbered giving employees their own personal road map. These numbers are used to announce the contest. This encourages readership of the contest because those numbers identified are instant winners. Additional winners are randomly selected from those who participate in the contest.

RESULTS

Through focus groups the TQM Road Map has been identified as a helpful communication device for raising awareness of the journey. The postcards have been identified as the single most successful communication device because they are clever and short. Participation rate in the contests has averaged about 250. The final measure of awareness of the three communication objectives will be taken in November.

LESSONS LEARNED

This promotional campaign has taught us that employees enjoy periodic, out-of-the-ordinary communication. Specific lessons learned include:

- **Keep it simple.**   Our initial contest was too hard. We spend a great deal of time verifying that the communication treatment would be favorably received by employees and did not spend the needed time on the actual content of the initial contest.
- **People did not see the personal connection or the need to keep the map.**   Although each map was individually numbered and this personalization was communicated, many employees did not keep the map. As each contest was launched, we continued to get requests for replacement maps.
- **The colorful approach encouraged the maps to be hung around the office.**   People saw the map as nice poster art to have in the work area.
- **Write-ups created informal pressure to produce results.**   The write-ups and results oriented postcards put some pressure on the teams to quantify their results for publication and personal recognition.
- **Initial fears of perceived "wastefulness" did not materialize.**   The concept testing suggested there would be some population that perceived the map as trite and wasteful. This was not the case or if it existed, it was by far the minority.

Deeds for Upper Managers:
Prepare Phase

As seen throughout this chapter, senior managers have key responsibilities for preparing their organization to embark on its

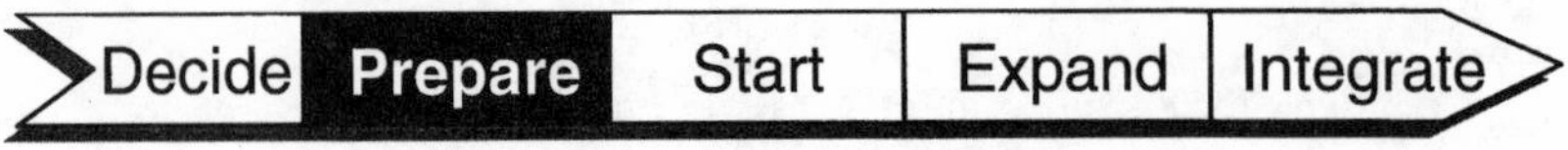

| >Decide | Prepare | Start | Expand | Integrate > |

Tasks for Upper Management

- Become trained in path chosen.
- Serve on Quality Council.
- Establish quality officer.
- Set initial goals and vision.
- Select pilot project(s).
- Establish pilot project teams.
- Establish assessment and planning task forces.
- Develop first-year plan in detail.

Figure 3.4   Upper Managers' Tasks: The Decide Phase.

quality journey. Figure 3.4 defines and addresses each of upper management's key tasks in the Prepare Phase.

As in Chapter 2, each of these "deliverables" can be viewed as a checklist item for respectively planning and reviewing senior managers' preparedness for launching their organizations on their quality journey.

HIGHLIGHTS OF CHAPTER 3

1. The purpose of the Prepare Phase is to ensure that the organization is ready to embark on its quality journey.

2. Senior managers require additional training in the concepts, processes, and tools they will need to fulfill their responsibilities for leading their organization toward total quality and for accelerating performance improvements.

3. Among the initial "deeds to be done" by senior management are: Organize and serve on a Quality Council that will choose pilot

projects; set policy, direction, and priorities; provide resources and review progress.

4. In choosing the pilot projects, senior managers can help ensure that the pilot teams receive the right training by understanding Juran's Trilogy of operational processes for managing quality.

5. Analogous to a Chief Financial Officer, the organization should appoint a Chief Quality Officer (CQO) to be responsible for designing the infrastructure required to implement the direction and policy of the senior managers.

6. Following the direction of the Quality Council, the CQO should organize and train selected middle managers to participate in the development and communication of:

   a. The rationale for the organization's quality journey.

   b. The plan and road map for the journey.

   c. The pilot projects that will be used to demonstrate the benefits to participants in the journey.

References

Bastian, R., and Miller, W. (1994). "Improving the Research Funding Process Through Process Management, Value Analysis, and Linkages to Other Processes—Lessons Learned," *Proceedings of Symposium on Managing for Quality in Research and Development*, Juran Institute, Wilton, CT.

Berry, T. (1991). *Managing the Total Quality Transformation*, McGraw-Hill, New York, NY.

Bolmey, A., McNab, P., and Yuhasz, N. (1992). "Kaiser Permanente: The Implementation of Total Quality Management in a Large Decentralized Health Care Organization," *Proceedings Juran Institute's IMPRO Conference*, Juran Institute, Wilton, CT.

Busch, J., Douglas, J., Montano, R., and Schulty, K. (1993). "Managing the Implementation of TQM at CSI," *Proceedings Juran Institute's IMPRO Conference*, Juran Institute, Wilton, CT.

Galvin, R.W. (1991). Interview in *Quality Benchmarks for Executives*, Videotape, Juran Institute, Wilton, CT.

Gunderson, R.L. (1993). "The Leadership Dimension to Launching Total Quality Management," *Proceedings Juran Institute's IMPRO Conference*, Juran Institute, Wilton, CT.

Howe, L. (1986). "Upper Management Leadership in Annual Quality Improvement," *Proceedings Juran Institute's IMPRO Conference*, Juran Institute, Wilton, CT.

Juran, J.M. (1992). *Juran on Quality by Design*, Free Press, New York, NY.

Juran, J.M. (1990). "Made in USA: A Break in the Clouds," Summary Address at The Quest for Excellence Conference, sponsored by the National Institute of Standards and Technology. Reprints available from Juran Institute, Wilton, CT.

Juran, J.M. (1989). *Juran on Leadership for Quality*, Free Press, New York, NY.

Juran, J.M. (1985). "IMPRO 85 Closing Remarks," *Proceedings Juran Institute's IMPRO Conference*, Juran Institute, Wilton, CT.

Juran, J., and Gryna, F. (1993). *Quality Planning and Analysis* (3rd Edition), McGraw-Hill, New York, NY.

Main, J. (1994). *Quality Wars*, Free Press, New York, NY.

McCain, C. (1995). "Successfully Solving the Quality Puzzle in a Service Company," *Proceedings Juran Institute's IMPRO Conference*, Juran Institute, Wilton, CT.

Wright, C. (1995). "TQM Road Map for Communicating Quality," *Proceedings Juran Institute's IMPRO Conference*, Juran Institute, Wilton, CT.

Zeidler, P.C. (1993). "Using Quality Functions Deployment to Design and Implement a Voice Response Unit at Florida Power & Light Company," *Proceedings of Symposium on Managing for Quality in Research and Development*, Juran Institute, Wilton, CT.

CHAPTER 4

Starting the Journey

Introduction

After preparing properly, an organization can embark on its quality journey more confidently. This chapter discusses the sequence of activities through which organizations ensure that their journeys successfully begin and continue. Examples of organizations' "kickoff" strategies and implementation tactics are provided throughout the chapter. These stories, from the "firing line," come from the senior and middle managers who have personally experienced and then generously shared them.

Defining Activities for the Start Phase

Figure 4.1 depicts the macrolevel activities contained in the Start Phase of the quality journey. It is crucial to concurrently undertake activities for conducting and supporting the pilot projects identified in the Prepare Phase, and the development, construction, and

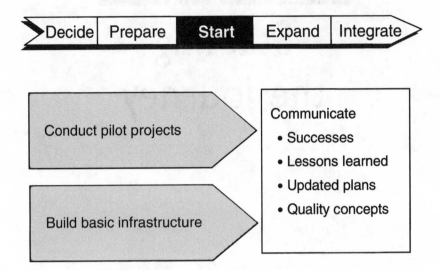

Figure 4.1   Macrolevel Activities of the Start Phase.

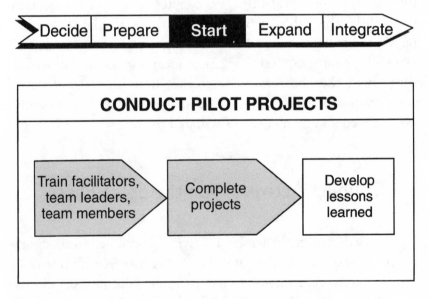

Figure 4.2   Tasks Associated with Pilot Projects.

review of the infrastructure required by the subsequent Expand Phase.

Conduct Pilot Projects

Figure 4.2 provides the tasks associated with the *Conduct pilot projects* macrolevel activity in Figure 4.1.

Train Facilitators, Team Leaders, and Team Members

Key questions to ask (and answer) before starting the pilot projects are:

1. What type of training should the facilitators, team leaders, and teams receive?
2. Who should provide the training?
3. When should the training be done?

The right answers to these questions will help ensure (1) the pilot projects' success and (2) a means to communicate and promote a successful start for the organization's quality initiative.

At Kaiser Permanente, Bolmey et al. (1992) decided on the following approach for training to support the Ohio Region's pilot projects:

For Team Leaders and Facilitators:

- "Team Leader and Facilitator Training"—5 days.
- "Tools for Quality Improvement"—5 days.

For All Team Members:

• "Quality Improvement Team Training"—2 days.

Training is provided on a "Just-In-Time" basis to teams. To date, over 200 employees have been formally trained in TQM philosophy and methodology, including 41 physicians and health professionals. This represents approximately ten percent of the Region's employees. Training is tracked via a PC-based tracking system, and its information is available to all training professionals in the Region.

Busch et al. (1993), at California Steel Industries (CSI) provided the following insights into the training of pilot project facilitators and team leaders:

The first improvement projects were developed from a brainstorming session of the Quality Council. There were 40 project nominations. This number was reduced to the eight deemed to be the most important by the Quality Council. Each project was of a cross-functional, or interdepartmental nature.

After the Quality Council selected its pilot projects for Quality Improvement Teams, they selected team leaders and facilitators for each project. The leader was generally the supervisor or manager of the department most affected by the project. The facilitator was matched to the leader with hopes that a good working relationship between the leader and facilitator would develop. These sixteen facilitator nominees participated in the Facilitating Juran on Quality Improvement and the Introduction to Quality Improvement Tools courses. An additional eight employees participated in the sessions, selected for their leadership and communication abilities, to help support the spread of TQM throughout the company.

Facilitating Juran on Quality Improvement taught the group a new way to think about quality. In addition to basic facilitation skills, the group learned the Quality Improvement Process, and practiced what they had learned in hypothetical circumstances. Introduction to Quality Improvement Tools taught the basics of each of ten different tools: when and how to use the tool, and how to interpret the results.

Both courses were held in-house during a two-week period.... The participants adjusted their schedules to allow them to continue regular duties while attending class eight hours each day. However, this experience helped CSI in future training sessions of leaders/facilitators; the following sessions were divided to assist the employees in maintaining their regular routines.

The teams attended a three-day workshop to learn the quality improvement process, working with their leader and facilitator. This gave them their first opportunity to work together while learning the quality improvement process and some of the basics of a few quality improvement tools. They were ready to go to work!

Complete Projects and Develop Lessons Learned

During the conduct and completion of the pilot projects, the Quality Council should regularly review the teams' progress and should encourage and support the successful completion of their projects. (The training the council members received during the Prepare Phase provides them with the knowledge required to determine whether the facilitators and teams are "in process.") Once the pilot projects have been completed, the facilitators, the Planning Task Force, and the Quality Council need to review:

1. What went right and why.

2. What went wrong and why.

Based on these lesson learned, they can then prepare the organization to replicate and expand the "right," and diagnose and remedy the "wrong." Concomitantly, the organization will avoid prematurely standardizing the infrastructure required in the Expand Phase. For example, McCain (1995), at Kelly Services, provided the following summary of what did and didn't work during the early implementation of Kelly's Quality Initiative:

What Worked

- Piloting the Quality effort on a smaller scale.
- Quality Advisors: Creating at least one Quality expert in each Kelly Enterprise area.
- Quality Partner Program: Assigning Quality experts to assist other organizations on their Quality journey.
- Quality Puzzle Awareness Program: Introducing Quality concepts and vocabulary to the Company in a progressive, non-threatening manner.
- Adoption Process: Instituting a program whereby organizations already in the Kelly Enterprise could not receive Kelly Quality Awards unless the organization adopted another organization just beginning its Quality journey. The adopting organization is deemed a Quality Partner.
- Executive Management support: Clearly communicating support and demonstrating leadership in the Quality initiative.
- Firm Quality goals and objectives: Allowing Kelly to remain focused and on track.
- Celebrating successes: Recognizing improvements from the top down.
- Statistical measures: Understanding that measures and Quality control plans can be applied to any business process.
- Quality Services Department: Ensuring that teams remained focused and dedicated to the Quality initiative.

- Quality System Adherence: Remaining focused (Kelly Enterprise members) on the criteria established by the Quality Services Department; using one Quality method.

What Didn't Work

- Forgetting the soft stuff: Implementing a Quality system involves cultural changes or changing the way people think about their jobs. Never lose sight of the influence cultural changes can have on an organization.
- Moving too fast: Beginning full-scale implementation before the Quality system foundation is built and enough resources are assigned to facilitate its development and implementation.
- Assuming everyone is at the same level: Developing ways to monitor the "depth" of Quality understanding is critical. Simply because everyone hears the same message, it does not mean everyone understands the message.
- Using Quality vocabulary too soon: Introducing Quality vocabulary slowly is critical.
- Training too soon: Conducting "just-in-time" training is important. People can lose skills they have learned if they do not have the opportunity to apply them immediately.

Similarly, Bartleson (1996) at the Mayo Foundation stated that:

Feedback from the initial team members included these observations/recommendations:

- Choose critical projects.
- Avoid jargon.
- Shorten training courses.
- Provide just-in-time training.
- Off-line work speeds progress.

- Communication between team and affected areas is critical.
- It takes too long!

The last comment, "It takes too long," is common for both the pilot and subsequent projects. Incorporating these and other organizations' lessons learned into future quality initiatives should help reduce the time from starting the pilot projects to successfully completing them. Bartleson (1996) also reported on working with Juran Institute and General Motors, respectively, to develop and implement a "blitz team approach" and the PICOS method (developed by General Motors):

Blitz teams use the same six-step process as regular quality im-provement teams, with the following differences:

- Preliminary meetings determine how the process works and data needs.
- Data must be available and some analysis conducted before team meets.
- Team meets for 2–4 hours twice a week for 4–6 weeks instead of 1–2 hours every 1–2 weeks for 8–12 months.
- Team leader and facilitator still required to do off-line work.

This approach requires that team members commit to lengthy meetings in advance and must, therefore, off-load some of their other responsibilities. One- to two-hour meetings every 1–2 weeks can be added to an individual's already busy schedule, but a 2–4-hour meeting cannot be "squeezed in." This change forced the institution to recognize the effort involved and support team members with dedicated time or replacements as appropriate. As noted, the blitz method mandates that data be available and par-tially digested before the team begins formal meetings. There is an extra benefit to the blitz approach in that improvements are implemented six months to a year sooner than would have occurred using a "regular" improvement team meeting schedule.

The following two examples illustrate the blitz approach in a clinical and an operational setting respectively.

The Stream Team

Problem: There is excessive variation in the care of patients undergoing radical prostatectomy.

Root Causes: Nursing (room) charges are higher if patients are admitted the night before surgery.

Anesthesia charges are higher with use of epidural infusion of medication for pain control.

Remedies: Develop ideal practice protocol for physicians and nurses.

Results: Length of Stay (LOS) reduced by an average of 1.8 days.

Reduced variation in practice.

Average savings of $2,000 per patient.

Added Benefit: Pain control equal with less expensive treatment and has fewer side effects, which allows patients to walk sooner.

Probable "spin off" benefit on other similar urologic procedures.

Return to Sender Team

Problem: It takes too long to process orthopedic disability claims.

Root Causes: Delays in Business Office.

Delays in receiving patients' charts.

Information is frequently not in chart.

Remedies: More efficient Business Office intake process.

Enter/Use information "on-line."

	Have clerk go to chart to abstract information.
	Leave focused note for physician if information is not in chart.
Results:	Average cycle time reduced by 68%.
Added Benefit:	Cycle time for all disability claims reduced by 57%.

Another expedited approach Mayo has used is called PICOS, Spanish for mountain peaks. This improvement method was developed by General Motors (GM). Initially, the PICOS method was used with suppliers to GM, then internally at GM, and is now offered to healthcare providers free of charge. GM is genuinely interested in improving the efficiency of the healthcare industry because the cost of employee medical benefits exceeds the cost of steel in U.S. cars. Healthcare is GM's largest outside cost. A summary of the PICOS method follows:

- Identify the area/process to be improved.
- Assemble a cross-functional, empowered team.
- Conduct initial process evaluation and data needs assessment/ collection.
- Team meets for three to four days to:

    —Fully understand current process.

    —Brainstorm and prioritize changes.

    —Determine measurements to monitor.

    —Implement immediate short-term and long-range improvements.

PICOS requires buy-in and approval from all key stakeholders. There is an immediate payoff from the effort, but full benefit requires follow-through on all elements of the implementation plan. This approach relies on the knowledge of team members regarding what "adds value" to a process. Waste and "non-value-added" steps are eliminated before and after measurement is conducted. In our setting, this approach has worked best when the process is under the control of a single department. Given appropriate leadership commitment, even greater results can be achieved through cross-departmental improvement efforts. While the initial PICOS teams have been facilitated by individuals from GM, we have trained Mayo personnel to facilitate future efforts. The following two PICOS teams illustrate the method.

West 17th Floor PICOS Project

Process Focus: One medical division's work activities—how patients are seen and managed in an outpatient setting.

Recommended Improvements: 117 total.

50 immediate (<1 month).

43 short-term (<6 months).

24 long-range (>6 months).

Examples: Eliminate counting of outside X-rays.

New "clinical assistant" position to assist patients and physicians.

Results: Patient waiting time dramatically reduced.

Daily review of test results eliminates unnecessary return visits.

Added Benefits: Patients really appreciate "family-like" atmosphere.

Staff morale much improved.

Human Resources PICOS Project

Process Focus: Data integrity in Human Resources Personnel Payroll Information System.

Recommended Improvements: 123 Total.

26 immediate (<1 month).

80 short-term (<6 months).

17 long-range (>6 months).

Examples: Provide training to suppliers of information for
                 database.

                 Eliminate unnecessary handling of paper forms.

Results: Improved accuracy of entered data.

                 Improved customer service/satisfaction.

Added Benefit: Recognized and met need for security system in
                 reception area.

Another approach to reducing both pilot project and follow-on projects' duration is to analyze the results of multiple projects to identify the primary factors contributing to unnecessary delays. Early and Godfrey (1995) summarized a multi-industry study of twenty quality improvement projects that were identified as "taking too long." Their study revealed:

- On average, for these projects, only 37 percent of the project time was actually needed (and hence 63 percent was wasted).

- Of the 63 percent of wasted time, 39 percent was attributable to management's not providing better "preparation and support," and 24 percent was attributable to teams' not using "best practices" when working on their projects. Among the more specific contributors to both of these areas are:

  - Limited time dedicated to the project.
  - Executives' delay in confronting resistance.
  - No previously existing measures (for baselines).
  - Vague mission.
  - Not sticking to the vital few root causes.
  - Too much flow diagramming too soon.
  - Conducting elementary training on team time.
  - Prematurely jumping to remedy.
  - Poor implementation planning (for proven remedies).

Build Basic Infrastructure

As discussed earlier, building an infrastructure is necessary to support the expansion of the quality initiative. Figure 4.3 identifies the two major classes of quality system infrastructure:

1. A process for the ongoing assessment of the organization's quality status (for identifying and prioritizing the next round of follow-on projects).

2. Processes (and organization) required to nominate, select, and support the follow-on projects, e.g., changing the current reward and recognition system to establish incentives for meeting quality goals.

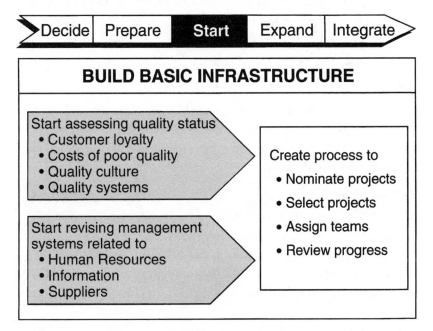

Figure 4.3 Building a Quality System Infrastructure.

Assessing the Organization's Quality Status

Juran and Gryna (1993) have used the term *Quality Assessment* to mean a *broad* review of an *organization's* quality status for use in understanding the "*size* of the quality issue," and identifying "the *areas* demanding attention." Their recommended activities for inclusion in quality assessments are:

1. Determining *Performance On Key Product Features Versus Competitors*. Requires the ability to determine, from an organization's customers (existing and desired), what features of its goods and services they most value, and, for each feature, how they rank the organization versus its competitors.

2. Estimating the *Cost of Poor Quality*. Focuses on the deficiencies dimension of quality. The organization must essentially answer the question: What costs would disappear if all of our key processes performed perfectly?

3. Characterizing the current *Quality Culture*. Aims to determine the underlying values, habits, and beliefs relative to quality that currently exist within the organization, and that may be either facilitating or impeding the successful completion of its quality journey.

4. Defining the *Quality System's* capability and performance. Identifies major opportunities to improve the efficacy of the organization's quality system, usually through utilizing one or more quality system standards (e.g., Baldrige or ISO 9000) for revealing the areas of the current quality system that should be prioritized for development or improvement.

Endres (1997) has provided examples of the use of each of these elements by various research organizations.

Gryna (1993), reporting on the role for the Chief Quality Officer, provides further insights into each of the dimensions of quality assessment:

An essential part of assessment requires opinions from the marketplace to learn how the quality of the company's product compares to the competition. Some of the main elements to address:

Quality Relative to Competition

- Identification of key quality attributes.
- Relative importance of key attributes.
- Status relative to competition.
- Effect of competitive differences on user.
- Creating a competitive advantage.

Realize also that understanding what the customer thinks of the quality applies not only to external customers, but also to internal customers. A few organizations have done the equivalent of marketing research on internal customers, with surprisingly good results. Examples of internal assessment from manufacturing industries include marketing research by a quality department and by an engineering design department to learn how the manufacturing internal customers view the services provided. Examples from service industries include marketing research done by a maintenance department to understand what the line organizations think of the quality of the provided maintenance services.

An old—almost half a century—and indispensable part of assessment is the cost of poor quality. Simply, this means an estimate of the amount of money being lost per year due to poor quality. [The following list] indicates where we must expand the traditional view of quality costs. Certainly the concept applies not only to manufacturing, but to all activities. For example, one engineering design organization assigns about 32% of the engineering personnel resources to find and correct design errors. In one service organization, one entire department exists only to locate errors in the transfer of charges between the organization's regions; the total budget of that checking department is slightly over one million dollars a year.

Cost of Poor Quality (The True Scope)

- All Processes, Not Just Manufacturing:
  —Product development.
  —Marketing.
  —Purchasing.
  —Billing.
  —Customer service.

Lessons Learned

- Emphasis on identifying opportunities for improvement instead of a scoreboard emphasis.
- Prevention, appraisal, failure structure is adaptable.
- Avoid undue precision.
- Express in meaningful language.

An Additional Dimension

- Effect of quality on sales income.

Recently, a message from the past has surfaced again: "It's too difficult to calculate the cost of poor quality." I fully disagree, and I speak from involvement with about 25 quality cost studies. We know the reasons for possible difficulty—desire for undue precision and a slavish adherence to defining quality cost in categories of prevention, appraisal, and failure costs (a useful structure but not in all cases).

Finally, the quality director must realize that the cost of poor quality is one dimension (cost) of the economic effects of quality.

The other dimension is the effect of quality on sales income. The first uses the quality improvement process; the second uses the quality planning process.

The third area of assessment gives us an understanding of the opinions, perceptions, beliefs, traditions, and practices related to quality for an organization—many of us tag this with the name "culture."

Organization Culture

Perceptions on:

- Management attitude on quality vs. production quotas.
- Quality of departmental inputs and outputs.
- Clarity of specifications, work instructions, and personal responsibilities for quality.
- Adequacy of feedback.
- Ability to regulate process.
- Obstacles to solving top problems.
- Management role model.

Many companies find it dangerous to draw conclusions about culture without collecting information from at least a representative group of employees. Collecting useful information requires that the objectives of the culture study be carefully defined, that the questions be pretested, and that other issues (e.g., distribution of results) be addressed. Focus group discussions, conducted by trained focus group leaders, can assemble this information. In other cases, companies make use of results obtained from carefully prepared questionnaires distributed to employees.

In many organizations, meeting production quotas on output is still more important than meeting quality objectives. The degree of seriousness of such a negative quality culture varies widely. At the serious end of the spectrum are the situations where people literally hide defective work. This occurs not only in manufacturing operations but also in other activities, such as software development (yes, software errors get hidden). If the boss wants a scorecard with good numbers, the boss will get one even if people have to destroy the system to achieve the numbers. Strong words—they do apply to some organizations.

These three types of assessment provide important snapshots of quality status. An additional form of assessment appraises the performance and results of the quality management system. Many companies apply the Malcolm Baldrige National Quality Award criteria or ISO 9000 for making this assessment. Whether done by a qualified outside organization or a trained internal audit group, an assessment to these criteria can create a new understanding of the strengths and weaknesses of an organization's quality system. The quality director, as consultant to executive management, must have a working knowledge of these criteria and the status of the organization in meeting them.

Example of Measuring Features' Importance

Jennison and Jordan (1991), of the Harvard Community Health Plan (HCHP), provided the following discussion on how HCHP organized to determine the key health care features as defined by its customers:

At Harvard Community Health Plan (HCHP), the Corporate Quality Council established a Customer Needs and Measures Advisory Council to develop a strategy for defining quality measures. It charged a group of quality professionals, market researchers, managers, and providers with responsibility for designing a comprehensive quality information system to support corporate-wide quality management. The Advisory Council, led by the Director of Quality

Management, Matt Kelliher, began with a systematic look at the HMO's customers and their needs.

The Advisory Council identified HCHP's customers as "current and prospective members (patients) and employers (purchasers)." Initially, the committee assumed that identifying customer needs and the HCHP's "product" would be equally simple. It soon became clear that each constituent on the committee had different interpretations of customer needs and the product definition. After considerable debate, the committee opted to hold focus groups with HMO members and purchasers to assess their needs and expectations of their health care provider. The net result was a consensus based on input taken directly from the customer. Hundreds of ideas from members were distilled into one basic product: Peace of mind that my family and I can get, or are getting, the best possible health care. This product translated into seven distinct categories of need:

Primary Customer Needs

1. Able to get care when I need it, conveniently.
2. The service I receive is personal and consistent wherever I go.
3. The care I receive is the best.
4. The health problem, or other reason for my visit, has been adequately addressed by the doctor.
5. Keep me informed on all aspects of my care.
6. No hassle; convenient and easy-to-use services.
7. At a cost which I should always be able to afford.

Once customer needs have been identified from the customers' perspective, the needs can then be translated into supplier terms—the provider's perspective of how the delivery system functions to meet customer needs. An example is [2. above] Patients need "consistent care" wherever in the system they are treated. At a more specific level, this need implies several different things, including a need to be handled consistently by all providers seen. From the providers' perspective, this refers to practice variation. Meeting patients' needs therefore implies reducing inappropriate practice variation. This can be measured by assessing the rate of noncompliance with clinical guidelines, standards, and goals that have been adopted by Plan clinicians.

While patients can identify what they need from providers, they cannot determine the high-priority diagnostic categories for which quality measurement and performance indicators are needed. Employers, however, can specify what they are purchasing and which services rendered to their employee population are of greatest interest to them. Employer groups are increasingly vocal and articulate customers of health care services. They are beginning to expect the same level of accountability from health care suppliers as they expect from their other suppliers of goods and services. A major example [below] defines the services of greatest concern to the Digital Equipment Corporation (DEC). This list defines the priority "products," from the purchaser's perspective, weighted according to Digital's expenditures for health care, short-term disability, and other external epidemiologic and utilization data....

Purchaser Priorities

Area of Interest	Weight
Mental Health	.26
Cardiovascular	.15
Musculo-skeleton	.14
Obstetrics	.08
Cancer	.08
Prevention	.08
Diabetes	.04
Respiratory	.03
Substance Abuse	.03

© HCHP 1991

Examples of Collecting and Utilizing the Cost of Poor Quality Data

Discussion of the collection of Cost of Poor Quality data for se-lected construction projects at a Spanish construction company, Dragados, has been provided by Moron and Ledbetter (1992). The data were collected "by project phase (design, construction, start-up) and project subelement (civil, mechanical, electrical, and the like). . . . Information is generated for management ac-tion, focusing on quality losses and improvement opportunities."

Rider (1996), at the Mayo Foundation, reported using Cost of Poor Quality data as a way to determine what and where were the largest opportunities to reduce costs:

> The Juran Institute proposed to us a Cost of Poor Quality Analysis of Mayo Medical Center Rochester as a way to sys-tematically estimate the amount and proportion of improve-ment opportunity with an economic payback. We had heard of the concept of the "third factory" from industry, that is, in any organization there is an embedded third factory of waste and inefficiency. Was this applicable to a medical organization like Mayo Clinic? We had to know the answer and an analysis was conducted. The primary methods of analysis used were: find-ing internal examples of highly efficient processes—internal best practices, external benchmark comparisons, and cost analysis. The most fruitful analytical approaches were internal comparisons of medical practice variation, benchmarking with two other large medical centers, as well as analysis of the under- and overutilization of costly resources (staff, equip-ment, and facilities). The study took four months to complete. The results were dramatic and eye-opening. There are signifi-cant opportunities with million of dollars of cost reductions. But more than the magnitude was the identification of where

the big opportunities were to be found. The biggest were not in the back-office, administrative-overhead areas (usually the first targets to look for waste) but in the core medical processes that comprise the bulk of what we do. True to the Pareto principle, 80% of the opportunities (the vital few) were in just four areas: variation in hospital practice, optimization of our large outpatient practice, increased hospital capacity, and the efficiency of our operating room services.

The largest opportunity was unexplained variation in use of resources for hospitalized patients. The analysis provided graphic demonstration of high variation in the use of such costly resources as laboratory tests, the intensive care units, medication, and length of stay. . . . The Cost of Poor Quality study was presented broadly throughout the organization and has stimulated the formation of 30 team-based improvement initiatives. . . . The analysis has provided a wealth of improvement opportunity and will result, we believe, in effective, intelligent, long-term cost reduction.

Examples Related to Quality Culture Studies

Juran and Gryna (1993) define an organization's quality culture as the "opinions, beliefs, traditions, and practices concerning quality." The quality dimension of an organization's culture results from the establishment and implementation of an infrastructure that drives *participation* in the organization's quality processes. Once employees reap the satisfaction of helping to improve their own and the organization's performance, they become motivated to perpetuate the changes in their opinions, beliefs, traditions, and practices. These changes, in turn, drive improvements in the organization's quality culture. To recognize the potential cultural impediments to successfully implementing quality initiatives, organizations are well advised to conduct focus groups and surveys of their current cultures. It is equally important to analyze, communicate, and then act on the results of the surveys. At Eastman Chemical Company, Holmes and McClaskey (1994) asked researchers to answer this question:

"Have you or your work group done anything to improve Research's effectiveness at developing and supporting new products and processes?"

Unfortunately, although the research organization had conducted training in quality concepts, processes, and tools, for several years, only 15 percent responded "Yes." Diagnosis of the responses revealed that their implementation had been focused almost entirely on *activities*, like the number of people trained in Design of Experiments, or the number of quality improvement teams. Instead, what was needed was a refocus of the quality initiative on *results* and the processes (e.g., reviewing the research portfolio) producing those results, which were directly related to the mission of the research organization. (When the survey was repeated in 1993, the percentage of researchers responding positively was 90 percent.)

French, reporting as Chief Operating Officer at the Inova Health System (French et al., 1993), discussed the use of a survey to identify gaps between Inova's desired characteristics for leaders and the actual perceptions of their direct reports:

Inova Quality Leadership Survey

The Inova Quality Leadership Survey is a tool designed to provide feedback to members of the executive and senior management teams regarding 30 specific behaviors. The consistent and continual demonstration of these behaviors by our leaders is considered necessary to support the establishment of the Inova Quality Leadership culture....

The initial survey form was piloted with three executive officers during the fourth quarter 1992. Changes were made based on feedback from the participants and observations made by members of the Inova Quality Leadership staff. The revised survey instrument was then completed by all fifteen executive officers during the second quarter 1993.

The survey process included three steps:

1. The completion of the instruments by each executive (self-perception) and 5–10 direct reports and/or peers (others' perception) on the same 30 behaviors.

2. A meeting between the executives and organizational development specialist to review the results and plan a feedback session with the survey participants.

3. A facilitated feedback session between the executives and the direct reports and/or peer groups regarding the results.

The data included self-perception scores and a composite score of others' perceptions regarding the executives' demonstration of these 30 behaviors. A variety of graphs were used to display the results and analyze the data. Then three basic approaches were used to analyze this information. First, gaps between the perceptions of the executives and others were analyzed either by question or general category. Second, overall low scoring areas were examined to understand what changes were seen as necessary. Third, general categories were looked at to determine how the frequency of the behaviors, while satisfactory, may be increased.

Since the data were based on individuals' perceptions, the facilitated feedback session was seen as an integral step in the process to enhance and clarify the understanding of people's actions. The desired primary focus of the survey process was this dialogue in the feedback session versus the scores received on the tool. The main purpose of the scores was to provide a mechanism to compare perceptions of behavior. Thus, these sessions afforded the opportunity for the executive to participate in direct discussion regarding his/her demonstration of these behaviors as well as to further evaluate the tool and process for future use and improvement. The results of this discussion also assisted the executive officers in identifying personal development goal(s) for their 1993 performance management plans.

Overall, this process was seen as an important part of further integrating a quality culture into Inova Health System. The following are general areas of improvement that we will focus on during the coming years as we expand the use of the Inova Quality Leadership Survey:

1. The current tool describes behaviors not understood, appreciated, and/or completely embraced by members of the senior management team.

2. Individuals need to feel secure in the feedback sessions and share feelings and observations without a fear of reprisal. This reflects the stage of our maturity within the quality journey and the need for additional development opportunities to support this endeavor.

The Inova Quality Leadership Survey process will undergo further refinements as it becomes a valued part of our cultural transformation.

Table 4.1 on page 100 provides the actual list of Quality Leadership Characteristics contained in the survey.

Assessment of Quality System

The current chapter covers the Start Phase in developing a quality system. Quality system assessment based on comparison with criteria—such as those contained in Baldrige, ISO 9000, state, or

Table 4.1 Leadership Behaviors for Driving Cultural
Change at Inova

Leads, teaches, coaches, and mentors others to continuously improve the
quality of care, services, and results through the daily use of Inova Quality
Leadership tools and techniques:

1. Creates and communicates appropriate Quality goals and objectives that
   uses Quality tools and practices in all activities as the primary means of
   improving recognized customer(s) satisfaction.
2. Manages by fact, to ensure that all outcomes and/or business decisions
   are supported by appropriately quantified data.
3. Establishes challenging team-based performance expectations and goals
   for continuous improvement based on an understanding of recognized
   customer(s) requirements and operational processes.
4. Exemplifies through personal behavior a model for daily work activities
   that encourages teamwork, empowers employee participation, drives
   out fear, and promotes personal and professional growth.
5. Enables and promotes learning, both for individuals and for management/
   department teams' members.
6. Uses a measurement process to monitor management/department team
   and individual performance goals on an ongoing basis, and provides
   timely coaching for improvement.
7. Leads by actions that demonstrate a constant quest for excellence by
   meeting/exceeding identified customer(s) requirement(s) rather than an
   avoidance of failure.

corporation quality standards—should therefore be used only to
identify and guide the development and deployment of those categories or elements of the initial quality system infrastructure that
have been identified in the Prepare Phase. However, because
many organizations use the Baldrige criteria in planning and
reviewing their existing quality systems, Tables 4.2 and 4.3 (on
pages 102–103) summarize the guidelines and process (from
Endres, 1997; described by McClaskey, 1992) used by the Eastman
Chemical Company (ECC) research organization.

Table 4.2 Hints for Effective Use of the Baldrige Assessment for Improvement

---

1. Keep executives/managers involved.
2. Stress/Reinforce using assessment to improve.
3. Link/Align with business objectives.
4. Integrate with existing business/improvement systems and cycles.
5. Promote external comparisons to be best.
6. Use award criteria without modification.
7. Require written applications, but give several write-up options, from "brief" write-ups to "full" 75-page write-ups written to Baldrige quality award standards.
8. Train managers/examiners/writers to understand the Baldrige criteria and assessment process.
9. Conduct pilot tests.
10. Avoid the "numbers game."
11. Stress cooperation and improvement.
12. Use Baldrige criteria for company quality awards. Give awards for improvement as well as meeting goals.

Examples of Quality System Infrastructure

Juran (1990) has summarized the importance of developing an infrastructure for the expansion and perpetuation of performance improvement:

> To meet stretch goals, the major form of "what to do different" consists of going into quality improvement at a revolutionary pace. The Baldrige winners did just that. Milliken reported that over 200,000 opportunities for improvement were implemented during 1989. Milliken also reported thousands of projects completed by action teams during 1989.

Table 4.3 ECC Research's Annual Baldrige Assessment
Process (1990–1991)

1. Evaluate and improve Research's Baldrige assessment process based on an analysis of the effectiveness of last year's Baldrige assessment.

2. Decide which units within Research will do their own Baldrige assessment, in addition to Research's overall assessment.

3. Set due dates for major milestones of the Baldrige assessment process.
   A. Due dates are set to integrate into the ECC improvement planning cycle.
   B. Process usually starts in April and ends in August.

4. When a unit is doing its own Baldrige assessment, the management team for that unit decides which Baldrige categories each management team member will personally write up and evaluate.

5. Provide training for everyone who will write up or evaluate any of the Baldrige items.
   A. A full day and a half-day of training initially.
   B. A refresher training session (2–4 hours) each year for those who had the initial training.
   C. Teach the Baldrige Award criteria and how to assess each Baldrige item using the Baldrige assessment scoring system. *Note:* The Baldrige criteria consist of categories that are further broken down into items and areas to address.
   D. Training should stress using the assessment to improve.

6. Individual members of the management team write up their selected Baldrige categories using a "brief" write-up format.
   A. The brief write-up format uses short phrases (bullets) to document the major points of each Baldrige item.
   B. Results items (Baldrige items that require data) are documented by either describing the relevant trends and levels, or by showing the data in chart form.
   C. All Baldrige items and areas to address are written up (based on the current year's Baldrige criteria).

7. The entire management team and the team's internal Quality Management (QM) consultant review all write-ups and make suggestions on how to improve the write-ups. The management team member who originally wrote up the category makes the needed changes to the write-up.

Table 4.3 *(Continued)*

8. Individual members of the management team personally evaluate each Baldrige item within their selected categories. In addition, the team's QM consultant evaluates all items.

   A. Evaluation includes, for each item, its strengths (+), areas for improvement (−), and percent score.

   B. Research evaluates its Baldrige write-ups using the same evaluation and scoring system that is described in the current year's Baldrige Award Criteria booklet.

9. The entire management team and the team's QM consultant review the Baldrige evaluations for each item, question the basis for the evaluation, and either accept the evaluation, or suggest changes. Suggested changes are incorporated into the evaluation, and the evaluation is then finalized.

   A. The evaluation results and score are not conveyed outside the management team and the unit that was assessed, except to pick up general strengths and areas for improvement.

   B. The management team plans how to share the Baldrige assessment with the rest of the unit that was assessed.

10. Based on the Baldrige assessment, the management team identifies the most important improvement opportunities.

    A. The vital few, most important improvement opportunities cited are based on the "areas for improvement" identified during the Baldrige assessment.

    B. Customer and business priorities and strategic plans are strongly considered when selecting the most important improvement opportunities.

    C. Immediate actions are initiated for any area in need of improvement that requires immediate attention (usually rare).

11. The improvement opportunities identified as most important during the Baldrige assessment are key inputs. They are considered, along with data from other sources (like customer interviews, Research people interviews, process data analysis, strategic plans, etc.), in developing next year's improvement plan for Research and for the unit that did the Baldrige assessment.

12. Repeat the entire Baldrige assessment process next year.

Xerox reported that 75 percent of employees were serving on manufacturing teams during 1990.

Those achieved results did not come free—they were a return on resources. A major category of those resources provided the infrastructure without which there would be few quality improvements.

Let me note here that to make improvements by the thousands requires quite an organized effort—an infrastructure. A process is needed for choosing the projects to be tackled. Teams must be organized and assigned to carry out the projects. The teams must be provided with a well-designed process for making improvements. The teams need to be trained in how to operate as teams, as well as in how to diagnose problems and provide remedies. Each improvement project requires multiple team meetings, and much homework between meetings. A review process is needed to monitor progress and to help teams which get stuck. Collectively it is a lot of work, and it requires corresponding resources.

Vanguard's Process for Project and Prioritization and Initiation

At the Vanguard Group, Berry (1992), while serving as a guest lecturer for Juran Institute, provided the author with the flow chart shown in Figure 4.4 and the matrix in Figure 4.5, developed and used respectively to nominate and prioritize projects for the Vanguard Quality Process (VQP).

The Citizens Process for Recognition

Another key dimension of a quality system infrastructure is the process used for rewarding and recognizing exemplary attainment

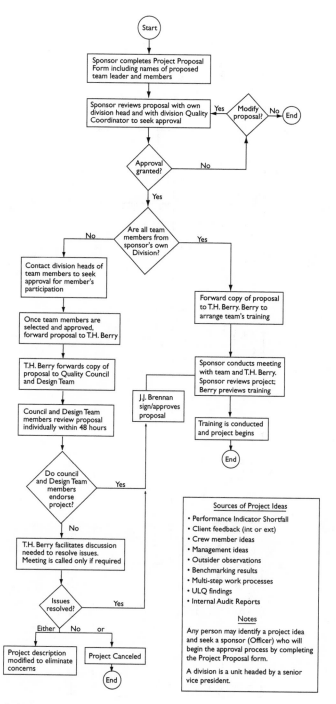

Figure 4.4 Vanguard's Project Initiation Process.

Project Idea: _____			Date:			
Use a 1 to 5 Rating Scale where 1 means low and 5 means high						
	Potential for Improving client satisfaction External? □ Internal? □ 1 2 3 4 5	Potential for Cost savings over 3-year period 100k 250k 500k 1 2 3 4 5	General importance or urgency 1 2 3 4 5	Potential for rapid completion >6 mos 4–6 <4 mos 1 3 5	Potential for replication of team results 1 2 3 4 5	Total Rating Remember to use weighting!
Factor Weighting	X 2 =	X 1 =	X 1 =	X 1 =	X 1 =	
Comments on Rating Factors						Decision: □ Approved □ Not Approved □ Study Further

Figure 4.5 Vanguard's Project Selection Matrix.

of individual goals that support the organization's goals for performance improvement. Taylor (1990), at the Citizens and Southern Trust Company, discussed the Citizens recognition process flow diagram shown in Figure 4.6. The recognition process was developed by a team of two middle managers and the Citizens Director of Quality Assurance (Taylor).

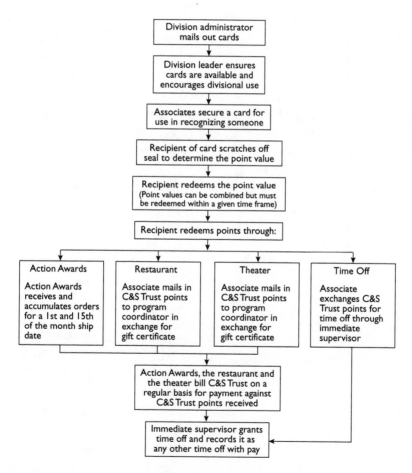

Figure 4.6 Citizens Recognition Process Flow Diagram.

Supplier Improvement and Management Processes at Alcoa and Toyota

The quality of an organization's products is a function of the quality of the goods and services it receives from its suppliers. Quaintance (1992), at Alcoa, described the rationale and process used to drive improvement in suppliers' quality:

> As the Aluminum Company of America (ALCOA) began to implement Total Quality Management (TQM) in 1988, the Procurement Department Quality Steering Committee asked me to develop a program to certify Alcoa suppliers. In December of that year I brought together a cross-functional team of representatives from procurement, quality assurance, and production departments to address the task. These representatives were from the corporate headquarters in Pittsburgh and from various Alcoa plants. During the next 14 months, the six-person Design Team and the facilitator met twice per month, for two days each time, to create the Alcoa Supplier Quality Improvement Process (ASQIP).
>
> Initially, the team's most important activity was benchmarking. The question that we asked the companies we visited was, "What do you do to improve the quality of the goods and services you purchase?" This is much broader than merely looking at certification programs, which, I might add, we also did. The responses led us to the conclusion that the most effective efforts were those that addressed improvements to the supplier's quality and management systems. The Design Team reported its findings to the steering committee and recommended that the team's mission be expanded from creating a certification program to developing a supplier quality improvement process. Approval was granted.
>
> The primary purpose of the ASQIP is to encourage and help suppliers to make continuous long-term quality improvements that

will ultimately contribute to the quality of Alcoa's products. We realize that our suppliers are critical to our success and make a significant contribution to our growth and competitive strength. The processes of our suppliers must be in control and capable for our processes to be in control and capable.

The ASQIP is designed to involve suppliers in the continuous quality improvement process, assess their quality awareness and competence, measure their progress of implementation, and recognize them for quality achievement. The process focuses on developing and implementing quality systems rather than auditing product quality. It is our contention that if the supplier's management and quality systems encompass the proper tools, disciplines, training, and tracking mechanisms inherent in quality, then the quality of the products and services will consistently meet or exceed the customers' expectations. The use of these systems must become the way business is done on a daily basis. . . .

Figure 4.7 is the process flow diagram developed by the Alcoa team to foster improvements in its suppliers' quality systems.

Toyota has also recognized the importance of working with its suppliers for "driving" improvements in their processes and products. Lampers (1993) provided the following description of Toyota's Supplier Development Program:

Uniquely to Toyota, I think our suppliers are an integral part of our manufacturing system. They are treated as partners in our production and marketing teams. Business relationships are intended to be long-term, and mutually beneficial. And they are based on the trust that grows out of experience.

In the past decade we've been working at Toyota Motor Sales to develop a cadre of well-qualified U.S. suppliers for the parts, accessories, and service parts needed by U.S. dealers and their customers. Each supplier must understand and act on the fact that customer needs, desires, and quality expectations

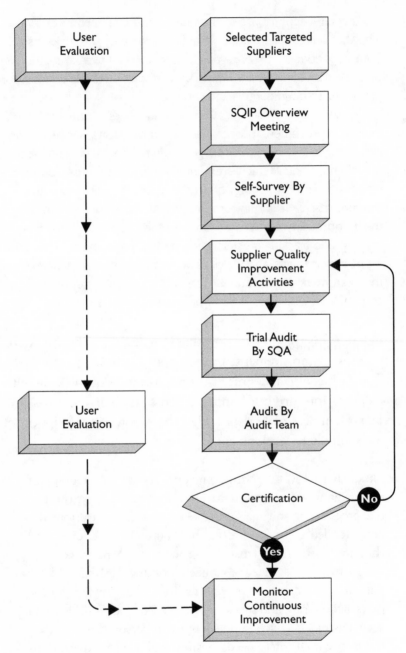

Figure 4.7 Alcoa's Process for Improving Suppliers' Quality.

drive Toyota's commitment to develop, manufacture, and sell the highest quality products.

When we talk about partnership with our suppliers, we mean pursuing mutual prosperity through mutual trust. The idea is to create relationships that lead to closer communication and expanded business opportunity—relationships that result in economic benefits to both parties.

Our strategy to develop U.S. suppliers with whom we can have such a "partnership relationship" is to communicate, educate, and motivate them to work with us in achieving our mutual goals. To help that process, we've evolved a comprehensive Supplier Development Program.

- In 1982, we began with an annual Supplier Seminar for the top management of supplier companies. It's a good forum for resolving problems and exchanging ideas, and we encourage two-way dialogue. This year, our suppliers themselves organized a second seminar to meet and discuss ideas of mutual interest.

- Our annual seminar was soon joined by the Toyota Quality Alliance evaluation program, which is the basis for our annual recognition and awards for the best suppliers.

- A more recently created evaluation tool, which we call a Supplier Capability Audit, not only focuses on our suppliers' history of excellence and long-term capability, but also their dedication to continuous improvement. These factors signal their potential for receiving new business in the future and for participating in our President's Challenge program.

- The President's Challenge was inaugurated four years ago. A number of suppliers have been invited to see the Toyota Production System in action at Toyota's plants and to meet and talk with some of our long-term Japanese suppliers.

- Two years ago, we launched our first full-scale Toyota Production System training program in the United States at Flex-N-Gate's truck bumper manufacturing plant in

Illinois. The Toyota Production System is often referred to as "lean manufacturing." Training companies to use the system is a major undertaking, but it really demonstrates the breadth of our commitment to supplier development.

- We've created a Supplier Committee composed of a core group of thirteen key suppliers who have demonstrated their long-term commitment to building the kind of partnership relationship Toyota desires.

- Also, two years ago, we inaugurated a series of seminars devoted to the implementation of TQM.

Start Phase: Roles and Responsibilities of Upper Managers

To lead and support pilot projects and infrastructure development, senior managers must understand and conduct the activities required during the Start Phase. Figure 4.8 is a summary of the tasks required for upper managers during the Start Phase.

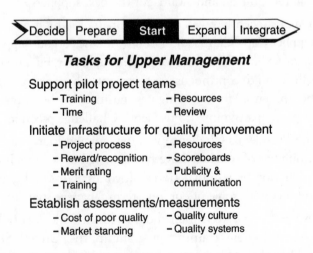

| Decide | Prepare | Start | Expand | Integrate |

Tasks for Upper Management

Support pilot project teams
- Training — Resources
- Time — Review

Initiate infrastructure for quality improvement
- Project process — Resources
- Reward/recognition — Scoreboards
- Merit rating — Publicity &
- Training communication

Establish assessments/measurements
- Cost of poor quality — Quality culture
- Market standing — Quality systems

Figure 4.8 Roles and Responsibilities of Upper Managers: The Start Phase.

HIGHLIGHTS OF CHAPTER 4

1. The Start Phase consists of two macrolevel activities:

   a. Conducting and reviewing results of the pilot projects selected in the Prepare Phase.

   b. Constructing an infrastructure of organization and processes for expanding and perpetuating performance improvement.

2. Key issues that must be addressed, before initiating the pilot projects, are: selecting and training team facilitators and team members.

3. Facilitators and team leaders need to be trained in team dynamics, project management, and the appropriate road map for the project, e.g., quality improvement, planning, or control.

4. To shorten projects' durations, team members should receive "overview training" in quality concepts *prior* to starting their projects.

5. Facilitators should provide team members with training in tools—e.g., Pareto analysis or fishbone diagrams—only as the members need them during the project.

6. Senior managers can help ensure the pilot projects' success and shorten their duration by:

   a. Ensuring team members are provided with enough time to dedicate to their projects.

   b. Confronting resistance quickly and consistently.

   c. Reviewing progress at key project milestones, e.g., identifying root causes.

   d. Recognizing the pilot team's accomplishments.

7. To build enthusiasm and participation, regularly communicate the status and progress of the pilot projects.

8. To avoid premature infrastructure standardization, review the pilot projects' results collectively.

9. Use task forces to design and develop individual elements of the infrastructure, e.g., project nomination and prioritization, reward and recognition, vendor development.

10. Use all dimensions of Quality Assessment (Performance on Key Product Features versus Competitors, Cost of Poor Quality, Quality Culture, Quality System planning performance reviews) to identify and prioritize follow-on projects.

References

Bartleson, J. (1996). "Major Results Quickly," *Proceedings Juran Institute's IMPRO Conference*, Juran Institute, Wilton, CT.

Berry, T. (1992). *Handouts at Juran Institute's Workshop on Total Service Quality*, Juran Institute, Wilton, CT.

Bolmey, A., McNab, P., and Yuhasz, N. (1992). "Kaiser Permanente: The Implementation of Total Quality Management in a Large Decentralized Health Care Organization," *Proceedings Juran Institute's IMPRO Conference*, Juran Institute, Wilton, CT.

Busch, J., Douglas, J., Montano, R., and Schulty, K. (1993). "Managing the Implementation of TQM at California Steel Industries," *Proceedings Juran Institute's IMPRO Conference*, Juran Institute, Wilton, CT.

Early, J., and Godfrey, A. (1995). "But It Takes Too Long . . . ," *Quality Progress*, American Society for Quality, Milwaukee, WI.

Endres, A. (1997). *Improving R&D Performance The Juran Way*, John Wiley & Sons, New York, NY.

French, M., Pittman, J., Stacy, R., and Wetjen, J. (1993). "Inova Quality Leadership—The Journey Continues," *Proceedings Juran Institute's IMPRO Conference*, Juran Institute, Wilton, CT.

Gryna, F. (1993). "The Role of the Quality Director—Revisited," *Proceedings Juran Institute's IMPRO Conference*, Juran Institute, Wilton, CT.

Holmes, J.D., and McClaskey, D.J. (1994). "Doubling Research's Output Using TQM," *Proceedings of Symposium on Managing for Quality in Research and Development*, Juran Institute, Wilton, CT.

Jennison, K., and Jordan, H. (1991). "A Quality Information System for Health Care TQM," *Proceedings Juran Institute's IMPRO Conference*, Juran Institute, Wilton, CT.

Juran, J.M. (1990). "Made in USA: A Break in the Clouds," Summary Address at The Quest for Excellence Conference, sponsored by the National Institute of Standards and Technology. Reprints available from Juran Institute, Wilton, CT.

Juran, J., and Gryna, F. (1993). *Quality Planning and Analysis* (3rd Edition), McGraw-Hill, New York, NY.

Lampers, A. (1993). "Toyota Partnering," *Proceedings Juran Institute's IMPRO Conference*, Juran Institute, Wilton, CT.

McCain, C. (1995). "Successfully Solving the Quality Puzzle in a Service Company," *Proceedings Juran Institute's IMPRO Conference*, Juran Institute, Wilton, CT.

McClaskey, D. (1992). "Using the Baldrige Criteria to Improve Research," *Proceedings of Symposium on Managing for Quality in Research and Development*, Juran Institute, Wilton, CT.

Moron, J., and Ledbetter, W. (1992). "TQM Start-Up in a Large Construction Company," *Proceedings Juran Institute's IMPRO Conference*, Juran Institute, Wilton, CT.

Quaintance, R. (1992). "Alcoa Supplier Quality Improvement Process Working with Suppliers," *Proceedings Juran Institute's IMPRO Conference*, Juran Institute, Wilton, CT.

Rider, C. (1996). "Focusing Improvement on What's Important," *Proceedings Juran Institute's IMPRO Conference*, Juran Institute, Wilton, CT.

Taylor, V. (1990). "Driving Corporate Objectives Through Recognition and Reward," *Proceedings Juran Institute's IMPRO Conference*, Juran Institute, Wilton, CT.

CHAPTER 5

Expanding the Gains

The previous chapter provided recommendations and examples for the sequence of activities that organizations should use to ensure that their quality journeys complete the Start Phase successfully. This chapter discusses the sequence of activities that organizations have used to expand the scope of their journeys. The purpose of the Expand Phase is to expand and accelerate the paybacks resulting from the initial investments in the pilot projects and the development of the quality system infrastructure.

Defining Activities for the Expand Phase

Figure 5.1 provides an overview of the Expand Phase's activities and their sequencing. Note that expansion takes place simultaneously in several dimensions. These dimensions include: the number of projects, the types of projects, and the types of teams. As will be seen, the new projects are expanded to include all three

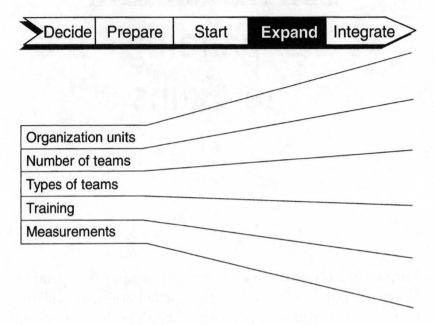

Figure 5.1 The Expand Phase (Macroview).

operational processes of Juran's Trilogy: Quality Planning, Quality Control, and Quality Improvement. Concomitantly, the scope of both training and measurement is enlarged to prioritize and support areas for accelerating the results stemming from the new teams' activities.

Expanding the Scope of Organizational Coverage

To paraphrase Juran, it is difficult, if not impossible, to get organizations to march in a uniform front. (Therefore, another useful criterion for pilot project selection is that the projects preferably

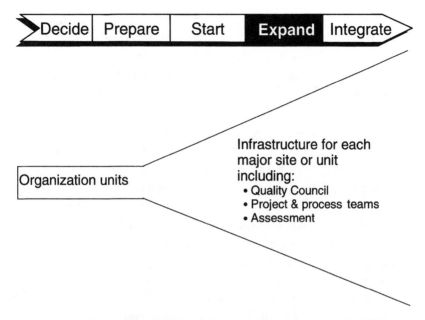

Figure 5.2 Expanding Organizational Coverage and Infrastructure.

be chosen from those organization elements that *volunteer* to participate in the initial round of quality improvement projects.) The success of the pilot projects is crucial not only for demonstrating the efficacy of the organization's quality initiative, but also for stimulating additional participation in follow-on projects. Figure 5.2 provides further insight into the scope of the organizational expansion.

Each new major organizational unit or division to be included in the scope of the quality initiative will train and organize a Quality Council, which will identify and prioritize its pilot projects and direct the ongoing assessments needed for the unit's subsequent projects.

At British Telecom (BT), Young (1990) reported on using a training process for BT's senior managers that:

. . . was adopted as the core design through a cascade process from the top team down through the layers of 43,000 managers. . . . and there are two important outcomes which are taken back to the ranch. The first is an individual senior manager personal action plan, which will enable improvement towards the BT Values and subsequent role modeling. The second is an idea for a personal project around which a team can be formed. . . . On return to the ranch, a Quality Council is formed to manage Total Quality Management implementation through Quality Improvement Plans and to stimulate the drive for continuous improvement. And so the process of cascade continues with each senior manager first attending a workshop, and then leading one for his/her own people. By this means, a hierarchy of Quality Councils is formed. . . . Not all of this has been easy. It has taken 3 years to cascade this process carefully through the management chain. During this time, nonbelievers certainly emerged— "Why do I need to change when the old system got me where I am?" is a popular excuse. However, with good facilitation and active role modeling by senior management, the principles can gradually be embedded. Converted cynics make good assets—make use of the domino effect.

The model of cascading councils has also been discussed by Braid (1988) at AT&T, Joines (1994) at Eastman Chemical, and Stratton (1992) at Storage Technology. Stratton reported:

The Excellence Through Quality management network establishes the basic leadership structure for implementing our plan. The network begins at the very top with our Chairman, President and Chief Executive Officer Ryal Poppa, who chairs the highest level process improvement council. Our executive vice presidents, vice presidents and directors chair their own process improvement councils, and we have quality officers worldwide (this idea borrowed from Alcoa). Quality officers are in every major division and foreign subsidiary around the world. Their roles are to communicate with the corporate quality organizations and network throughout the entire world to assure that Excellence Through Quality is implemented in an expeditious manner.

Expanding the Number and Types of Teams

When the initial round of projects is completed, the infrastructure designed for selecting and supporting teams during the Start Phase—e.g., the assessment and project nomination processes—is used to expand both the number and types of teams. Figure 5.3 portrays this dimension of the Expand Phase.

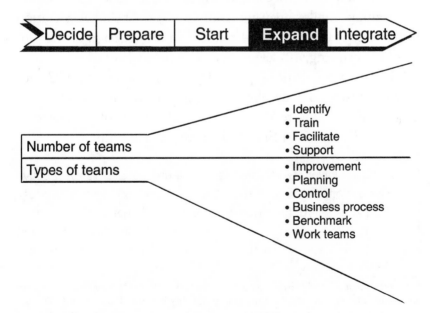

Figure 5.3 Expanding the Number and Types of Teams.

Because we have previously discussed the elements of infrastructure contained in the upper portion of Figure 5.3, we'll now
examine how organizations have used other types of teams—e.g.,
Planning, Control, Business Process—contained in the lower
portion of the figure.

Quality Planning Teams

After completing pilot quality improvement projects, organizations are encouraged to include quality planning projects in their
next round of projects. As discussed in Chapter 1, Juran's quality
planning process is associated with the "features" dimension of
quality. Operational quality planning projects typically result
from a recognized need for either a *nonexisting* product or process,
or a complete reengineering of an *existing* product or process.*
For example, a pilot quality planning project at Aid Association
for Lutherans (Morse, 1996) resulted in the redesign of the process for recruiting and selecting AAL's field agents.

The following IMPRO paper, by Mason and Long (1992), focused on the need to develop a set of design requirements for vendors' bids on the redesign and development of a new cost
accounting process for Stanford University Hospital:

> Stanford University Hospital formed a unique and highly effective
> organizational structure to support its quality planning process.
> This paper will define the key aspects and benefits of that struc-
> ture. It will also discuss the cost accounting quality planning process
> that took place within this organizational framework. The cost

---

* The text, *Juran on Quality by Design* (Free Press, New York, 1992), provides an extensive
discussion of Juran's Quality Planning process. Quality Function Deployment (QFD) is a
tool for organizing the data required to complete the steps of Juran's Quality Planning
Road Map.

accounting quality team approached the process with a thorough understanding of the cumbersome tasks hospital personnel were faced with in attempting to extract cost-related information from the hospital's computer systems. At Stanford University Hospital, variable costs are determined using departmental ratios of costs to charges (RCCs). Each year as a by-product of the budgeting process the hospital's Department of Financial Planning and Analysis updates these RCCs. Analysts search the decision support system for the appropriate inpatient population and run a program which lists revenue by cost center. [These data are] entered into a spreadsheet that contains the RCCs and calculates the variable costs. All other types of costs must be manually tallied and added to the analysis. Because this process is highly labor-intensive, it is completed on an infrequent basis.

Through the Juran quality planning process, the cost accounting team determined basic specifications for a system to meet the needs of the hospital's Department of Financial Planning and Analysis and its customers. The team developed functional specifications, determined data elements, and identified critical interfaces required of a cost accounting system. These requirements were incorporated into a request for information that was distributed to potential system vendors.

The Planning Process: Organizational Structure

Stanford University Hospital's Quality Council, made up of 10 senior hospital managers and the Deputy Chief of Staff, selected a series of quality planning projects that would improve management information systems to support decision-making processes. In all quality improvement and planning processes undertaken at the hospital, the Quality Council is responsible for defining projects, choosing teams, assigning missions, reviewing interim and final reports, and providing support as needed.

Because the council wanted to ensure that the hospital's overall system needs were analyzed and addressed in an integrated manner, multiple quality planning teams for decision support systems were concurrently established. The teams, comprised of major users of the desired functions, were responsible for undertaking specific quality planning projects. Communication among groups was important in order to create consistent solutions and reduce potential redundancies. It was also important for teams to communicate their needs to one another, as some groups were users of other teams' data and information.

Four planning teams were formed, representing cost accounting, managed care (contracts), department management reports and service lines. Another team entity was established to bridge the organizational gap between the planning teams and the Quality Council. This group, called the Decision Support System Coordinating Team, was formed to plan the overall decision support system that would meet customer needs. Fourteen members were included on the coordinating team, which included one to two delegates from the Quality Council and from each of the four planning teams. One facilitator was chosen to serve on both the coordinating team and the four planning teams (Figure 5.4).

The coordinating team played an important role throughout the planning process. However, their key responsibilities came into play at the end of the process when each planning team's final results and conclusions were transferred to the coordinating team. The coordinating team then analyzed potential systems and vendors, considered overall system needs, determined next steps, and completed a request for information documents for distribution to potential vendors.

The coordinating team created a dictionary of terms for defining data elements. This dictionary was referenced and applied by each planning team as they developed the system's product and process features. The facilitator helped ensure that common language was used by each team in order to create clear and consistent end products.

Throughout the planning process, the coordinating team made sure that the planning teams were working toward the same goals.

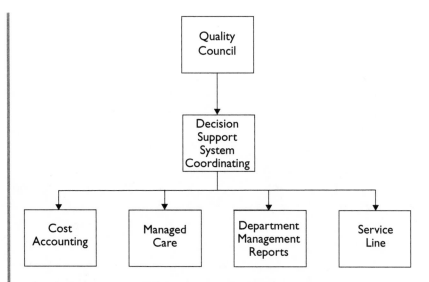

Figure 5.4 Quality Planning Infrastructure at Stanford University Hospital.

At the end of the process, the coordinating team possessed the expertise, organizational and financial backing to implement a program to create a master system that would meet the needs of each planning team and its customers. After creating the request for information in January of 1992, the coordinating team interviewed potential vendors, conducted site visits, and chose a vendor to implement the systems project.

At the start of the project, the Decision Support System Coordinating Team defined its problem statement as: "A decision support system that meets customer needs does not exist." The mission statement was: "To plan for a decision support system that meets customer needs."

The unique and highly effective organizational structure that Stanford University Hospital set up to support its quality planning process helped enable all teams to reach their individual missions and ensured that the common mission of creating a decision support system consistent with customer needs was met.

The remainder of this paper will discuss one team's quality planning process that took place within the hospital's organizational framework.

Of the four teams, the cost accounting team moved through the process the fastest. Positive group dynamics helped the group achieve its goals. The team included a dedicated group of six experienced hospital personnel—who clearly had mutual respect for one another. A well-defined objective and consistent application of the Juran process also contributed to the team's success.

Since the cost accounting team finished each step in the planning process before the other teams, they were able to continuously share what they had learned. The team leader played a key role in moving the team down the planning path by developing agendas, planning next steps, making assignments, and keeping the team and its duties organized. Other cost accounting team members included representatives from the hospital's Finance, Hospital Administration, Business Development, Contracts, and Nursing departments.

The cost accounting team defined the problem they were to address as: "A cost accounting decision support system that meets customer needs does not exist." Their mission was: "To plan a decision support system that meets customer needs for cost accounting."

There was a widespread perception within the hospital that an improved cost accounting system was needed. People were asking for more and more cost-related types of information. After downsizing occurred at the hospital, it became necessary for all departments to manage their budgets more closely and to determine innovative ways of lowering costs. Because the hospital had also embarked on a volume-building campaign, the demand for rapid turnaround on business proformas and reviews had increased.

However, it was difficult for the departments to obtain an accurate picture of actual and historical costs. An improved cost accounting system would provide the types of information needed to support each department's decision-making process. It would also make the overall budgeting and business planning process less burdensome. A key element of the hospital's approach to budgeting and cost analysis is the development of ratios of costs to charges (RCCs). The Department of Financial Planning and Analysis, in conjunction with the appropriate department managers, is responsible for updating the RCCs.

These RCCs were used to determine variable costs—through a highly labor-intensive process. The staff selected an inpatient population using various data elements. A program, which listed gross revenues by cost center, was then run. These data were entered into a spreadsheet containing the RCCs. The variable costs were calculated. Other costs associated with the patient population had to either be manually calculated or estimated. Corresponding outpatient information was unavailable through the system and therefore, also had to be manually collected.

Although cost centers estimated variable and fixed costs in total, the hospital's system did not contain the necessary information or features for detailed, procedure-level cost accounting and budgeting. However, competing hospitals either had, or were in the process of installing, cost accounting systems that allowed for efficient and effective decision making. Stanford University Hospital's management feared that the hospital's lack of such a system was a competitive disadvantage.

Identifying Customers

During one of their initial weekly meetings, the cost accounting planning team identified their customer groups. They determined that the vital few customers were Business Development, Contracts, Service Line Management, and Department Managers.

The useful many customers included:

Administration	Quality Assurance
The Board of Directors	Case Management
Financial Planning	Children's Hospital
Data Entry Billing Clerks	Payroll
Nursing	Accounts Payable

Other areas associated with generating/processing charges:

Materials Management   General Accounting

Healthcare Financing   Third-Party Payors

Administration   Hospital Management
                                        Information Services

State Government   The Public/Patients

Employers   Patient Financial Services

The team developed a flow chart that described the steps in the cumbersome process the Department of Financial Planning and Analysis was undertaking in order to calculate variable costs. The steps were defined as:

1. Define population by user-defined criteria.
2. Break out total gross charges by cost center.
3. Walk spreadsheet to financial planning.
4. Apply RCCs.
5. Add direct cost of population/program.
6. Produce income statement of population/program.

Discovering Customer Needs

To discover customer needs, the team asked the key customers they had previously identified to attend team-facilitated brainstorming meetings. As an output of this process, the team was able to capture the distinct needs of each user group. The team encouraged participants in the brainstorming process to avoid thinking about what couldn't be done. Users were asked to focus on what they truly wanted and needed—despite any perceived limitations. The team recorded needs by customer segment in a spreadsheet format (Figure 5.5). Column by column, they began building a picture of the cost accounting system that would meet those needs. (See first column: "Needs.")

The team sought customer input from management representatives within various departments, including nursing and ancillary

PRODUCT DESIGN SPREADSHEET
PAGE I

QMP TEAM: Cost Accounting
CUSTOMER: Business Development

PRODUCT FEATURES

Needs	Translation	1	2	3	4	4A	5	6	6A	7	8	9	10	11	12
		Training Sessions	Capacity for More Identifiers (Subacts. & Cost Ctrs.)	Multiple Data Elements for Each Procedure	Download Info for Local Processing	Download Info for Local Processing	Access to Daily Info	On-Line Access for Users	On-Line Access for Users	Ability to Aggregate by Multiple Variables	Modeling Capability	Coordin. & Commun. on Chg. of Subacct. Usage	Multiple Wgted. Wk. Units for Each Dept.	Standard Costs	Incremental Institution Costs by Contract
Prospective Costs	Modeling Capability Based on Historical or Std. Information									H	H				
Costs by Nursing Unit	Costs by Day Broken Down by User Defined Variables		H	H						M					
Finer Breakdown within Departments	More Cost Centers		L												
Costs by Procedure	Cost by Discrete Unit of Service(s) or Supply(ies)		H											H	
On-Line Access to Information	On-Line Access to Information							L							
Identify Who Customer Is for Procedures or Cases	Aggregate Costs for Proc./Episodes by Collected Variables Assoc. w/Pt.			H						H					
Reimbursement Rates by Procedure or Episode	Expected & Actual Reimbursement by Procedure or Episode									M					
Download Information for Local Processing	Download Information for Local Processing				H										
Cost per Total Episode	Cost of Clinically Defined Time for In & Outpt. Care Exc. Unrel. Care/Srvs.			H			H			M	M			H	
PRODUCT FEATURE GOALS		Qtrly. on Fn'l Rpt. Subaccts. & Cost Ctr.	Capacity for Unltd. User Defined Variables	Capacity for Unltd. Elements User Def. Variables	Download to ASCII Format	Download from System of Origin	Attach Date of Service to Each Variable	Query System of Data Origin	Access Data on Real Time Basis	Unlimited Ability to Def. Subset of Element by User	Ability to Apply Math/ Forcst. Tools	Annual Eval. of Exist. Pol. & Proc. Stmts.	Unltd. Types of Wk. Units & Aggregate	All Cost Accting. Data Elements	Inc. Increm. Institution Costs into Contract GRP Costs

Figure 5.5 Product Design Spreadsheet.

departments. Each department had specific needs, although some sought common system features and capabilities. In general terms, department managers wanted the system to provide information on costs (by patient type/procedure and per various time frames) and personnel productivity (actual versus standard hours per unit of output, etc.). They also wanted to be able to easily compare various reports.

Business Development was primarily interested in prospective and current costs (by department and procedure) and customer-related information.

The Contracts department's informational needs were related to profits and losses, costs (by patient, case type and per various time frames), and service dates. They also wanted the system to provide information that would allow them to gauge the operational impact of various contract requirements.

Translating Needs

As a group, the team translated the customer needs they had gathered into common terms (see Figure 5.5, second column). The dictionary that the coordinating team had developed was useful in this process. As questions or concerns about definitions were raised, they were recorded by the facilitator, who took them back to the coordinating team to be discussed and resolved.

Developing and Optimizing Product Features

The team discussed and listed their perspectives on the capabilities (product features) the system would need to have in order to meet the translated needs. They then ranked the importance of each feature in relation to each need. (See Figure 5.5, columns 1–12.) To ensure that the ranking process was objective and consistent, the cost accounting and coordinating teams developed the following definitions of the terms "High," "Medium," and "Low":

- High—Must have to do your job.
- Medium—Essential, but otherwise available with effort.
- Low—Nice, but not essential.

In determining product features, the group considered what features the system could realistically perform. To ensure that the product's features would meet customer needs, the team developed a series of product (feature) goals. These goals also served as milestones by which to measure progress during the system implementation phase. As the team considered various needs, features, and goals, they concluded that many features and goals were the same from one need to the next. They began to see relationships among needs as they identified common features and goals.

The team's product features and goals were plugged into a second spreadsheet (Figure 5.6) that would be used in designing process features.

Developing and Optimizing Process Features

Next, the team defined process features—the initial steps that would have to be accomplished in order to reach their product goals. Because it was exciting to put the group's thinking into actionable terms, the process features were enthusiastically developed through a less lengthy and complicated meeting than the group had experienced before. Finally, the group was talking in nontechnical terms to which everyone could relate. After the meeting, the process features were added to the design spreadsheet. (Figure 5.6 is a sample page from the Process Design Spreadsheet.)

Outputs of the Cost Accounting Quality Planning Process

Early in the planning process, the cost accounting team recognized the need to separate discussions on (1) system features/functionality (how the system operates) and (2) data elements (system inputs and outputs). The team also recognized the common industry

PRODUCT DESIGN SPREADSHEET
PAGE I

QMP TEAM: Cost Accounting

			PROCESS FEATURES												
		1	1a	1b	1c	2	3	4	5	6	7	8	9	10
Product Features	Product Goals	Develop Program	Develop Program	Develop Program	Develop Program	Develop GL Evaluation Criteria	Review Currently Collected Data	Conduct Needs Assessment for New Data	Develop Download Procedure w/Security	Define Date of Service	Collect and Store Date of Service	On-Line Data Entry for All Systems	Timely Update of Pt. Charges	Access for All Authorized Users
Training Sessions	Quarterly Training Sessions on Fin'l Rpts., Subaccts. & Cost Allocation	X	X	X	X									
Capacity for more Identifiers	Capacity for Unltd. User Defined Variables	X	X	X	X	X								
Multiple Data Elements for Each Procedure	Capacity of Unltd. No. of Elements, User Defined Variables						X	X						
Download Information for Local Processing	Download to ASCII Format								X					
	Dwld. from Syst. of Origin i.e., Payroll, Census &/Or Cost Accounting								X					
Access to Daily Information	Attach Date of Service to Each Variable									X	X			
On-Line Access for Users	Query System of Data Origin								X				X	
	Access Data on Real Time Basis								X	X		X	X	X
Ability to Aggregate by Multiple Variables	Unltd. Ability to Define Subset of Elements by User						X	X		X		X		
Modeling Capability	Ability to Apply Mathematical & Forecast Tools								X					
Communication & Coordination on Change in Subaccount Usage	Annual Eval. of Existing Policies & Proc. Stmt. Reinforced in Trning. Sessions	X	X	X	X									
		Curriculum Set	Classes Scheduled for Time & Place	Instructors Assigned	Evaluation Criteria Developed	Assess Current GL	Determine Which Are to Be Stored Long Term	Develop List of New Data Elements	Document Steps w/ Screen Design	Instruct Data Entry & Collection Personnel on Definition	Date of Service Attached to Service Code/Proc.	No More Batch Entry of Chg. Slips	Patient Charges Accurate to Each Midnight	Access through Any User Terminal
						PROCESS GOALS								

Figure 5.6 Sample Page from Process Design Spreadsheets.

terms that should be used in the request for information for distribution to potential systems vendors.

When the team was asked to provide a set of information detailing the basic specifications for a system to meet the needs of the Department of Financial Planning and its customers, they:

- Summarized the recommended features in the form of general, spreadsheet, graphics, mathematical, and report design "functional specifications."
- Listed the needed data elements.
- Described critical interfaces among hospital systems.
- Included the results of interviews and brainstorming sessions with the vital few customers.

Throughout the planning process, the team leader was careful to always instill a clear mission and focus in the team. However, that focus did not prevent the team from raising and capturing innovative solutions that, while outside the scope of the project, were highly valuable to the hospital. The cost accounting team transferred to the coordinating team and Quality Council a set of recommendations they had identified during the planning process. Many of the recommendations entailed forming additional quality planning and improvement teams to resolve key information systems issues the team had observed.

Internalization and application of the Juran process enabled the cost accounting quality planning team to create the specifications for an optimal cost accounting system. It also allowed them to add tremendous value by identifying improvements related to the hospital's overall information systems.

Quality Control Teams

In Chapter 1, we discussed Juran's Quality Control process in the context of the Juran Trilogy. The macrolevel steps for this process were provided in Table 1.4. Juran Institute has named the procedure for implementing quality control for departmental processes *Quality for Work Groups* (1992). Figure 5.7 is a high-level flow chart of Juran Institute's implementation procedure.

Similar implementation procedures have been developed and used by Florida Power and Light and the Vanguard Group. They have been titled, respectively, "Quality in Daily Work Life" (Walden, 1986), and "Unit Level Quality" (Brennan, 1991). An

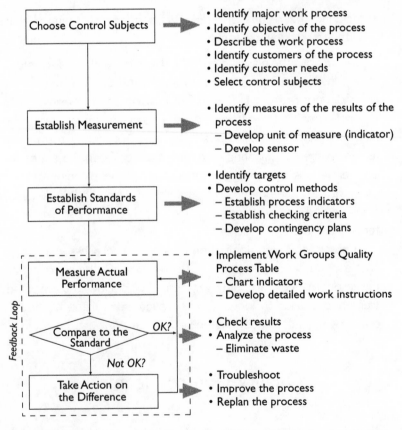

Figure 5.7 Juran Institute's Quality for Work Groups Implementation Flow Diagram.

important objective for any of these procedures is to expand participation in the organization's quality initiative to the department/unit level.

The primary focus of the Quality for Work Groups process is to implement quality control. However, within the "feedback loop," when it becomes necessary to determine the cause(s) for not meeting the "standard" or goal, the investigation *may* lead to either a quality improvement or a quality planning (reengineering) project that will not only reduce variation, but will also improve the *average* performance level. For example, Satterthwaite (1995), Director, Corporate Financial Management, at the Vanguard Group, reported that a unit-level team addressed the time it took for Vanguard to issue a replacement check. Replacement checks had to be issued when customers' original checks had been lost or stolen. "After the team's recommendations were implemented, the average time to issue a replacement check went from 3.5 days to 1 day, *and the range went from 1 to 27 days to 1 day.*"

Business Process Teams

Juran (1995) has referred to "Business Processes" as "multifunctional–horizontal macroprocesses through which [organizations'] work gets done." These processes are typically related to one or more critical success factors and derivative elements of strategy that the organization needs to accomplish in order to fulfill its mission. Examples of typical Business Processes include the product development process, purchasing, order processing, and product distribution. Figure 5.8, from Juran Institute's *Re-Engineering Processes for Competitive Advantage (Business Process Quality Management)* (1994) exemplifies the alignment of key business

Functional vs. Process
Management System

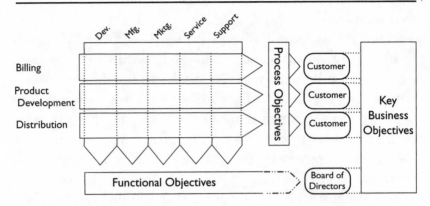

Figure 5.8 Example of Aligning Organizational, Business Process, and Functional Objectives.

process and functional objectives with the key objectives of the organization.

Figure 5.9 is Juran Institute's macrolevel road map for implementing Business Process Quality Management (BPQM) within any organization. Imbedded within the "Initiate BPQM" block are two key BPQM elements that distinguish Business Process teams from Quality Improvement teams:

1. Each business process has an executive owner (usually, a Quality Council member).

2. Business Process teams are permanent.

Within Phase Three of the road map, Juran's Trilogy of operational processes for managing quality is used for ongoing improvement and control of the key business processes after the Business Process teams have transferred the results of their projects to operations.

Road Map for Managing Business Process Quality

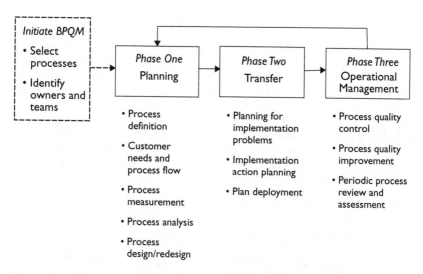

Figure 5.9 Juran Institute's BPQM Implementation Road Map.

The following financial services example, presented by Hooyman and Lane (1995), provides AAL's tailored version of Juran Institute's Business Process Quality Management road map, plus tools and lessons learned from implementing BPQM at the Aid Association for Lutherans:

> This paper explains how a pragmatic mechanism, AAL's BPQM road map, is being used to integrate proven techniques from several disciplines to meet business process reengineering (BPR) project objectives at Aid Association for Lutherans (AAL). It was developed based on lessons learned from initial BPR projects and leverages the strengths of various analysis disciplines including: Business Process Quality Management (BPQM), Information Engineering (IE) and Cost of Quality (COQ). Exhibit I (Table 5.1) provides a brief description of each of these disciplines. The road map

Table 5.1 AAL's Definitions of BPQM, Cost of Quality, and Information Engineering

Business Process Quality Management (BPQM)
This discipline provides a cross-functional focus on key business processes within an organization. These key business processes must be managed to maintain processing effectiveness across functional responsibilities, from beginning to end of the process. A process management team develops process measures to satisfy business and customer requirements, and manages the process using quality control and quality improvement techniques.

Some key business processes require radical changes—reengineering—to bring them in line with changes in customer requirements or to improve deteriorating process measures. A BPQM redesign project will analyze the existing process, reengineer the process, and perform ongoing process management to hold the gains and maintain the effectiveness and viability of the process.

Cost of Quality Analysis (COQ)
This discipline categorizes costs within a process into several groupings:
- Preventive Costs—associated with preventing or minimizing defects within the process.
- Appraisal Costs—associated with assessing process outputs for accuracy and completeness, to detect the existences of deficiencies.
- Failure Costs—associated with correcting defects or using defective output.
- Business Costs—those process costs not categorized as preventive, appraisal or failure costs.

An effective cost of quality analysis pinpoints where to redesign a process to:
- Eliminate major deficiencies.
- Trim major costs.
- Spin off quality improvement efforts to take care of smaller pockets within the process.

Information Engineering (IE)
This discipline is an interlocking set of formal techniques for the planning, analysis, design, and construction of information systems on an enterprise-wide basis rather than for a single project. IE progresses in a top-down fashion through the following phases:
- Strategic Information Systems Planning.
- Business Area Analysis.
- Business Systems Design.
- Business Systems Implementation.

IE creates a framework for developing a computerized enterprise. Separately developed systems fit into the framework. The enterprise-wide approach makes it possible to achieve coordination among separately built systems and facilities the maximum use of reusable system components.

concept can be adapted to meet any organizations project objectives. This paper highlights:

- How AAL tested some of the analysis tools on the first BPQM project, and then developed the road map to integrate them for subsequent efforts;

- How the road map works, and how it has been applied at AAL;

- How AAL selected team members and determined when to bring others in for support; how to keep everyone "in the loop"; and how to consider the impact on people when the redesign is implemented;

- How companies might adapt the road map concept for their efforts; how to use the right tool, at the right time, at the right level of detail, to meet project objectives.

BACKGROUND

Aid Association for Lutherans (AAL) is the largest fraternal benefit society in the United States, offering financial products and volunteer opportunities to more than 1.6 million Lutherans. Founded in 1902, AAL's financial products include life and disability income insurance, annuity and retirement products, long-term care and Medicare supplement coverage, a family of mutual funds offered through AAL Capital Management Corporation, and savings and loan products offered through AAL Member Credit Union. Through its operations based in Appleton, Wisconsin, AAL manages $14.8 billion in assets. Its 1,700 home office and 2,200 sales representatives work together with members to make a difference in their communities through fund-raising and service projects. AAL offers free educational materials for members on family and health topics, scholarship opportunities, and a wide range of grants to help Lutheran congregations and institutions.

AAL began its quality journey in 1991, building awareness of TQM principles before launching several quality improvement and quality planning pilot projects. A Quality Council was formed, consisting of the CEO and six division heads responsible for planning the TQM journey and championing each quality project. The Quality Council became interested in learning how to manage key business processes across all areas involved in the process. The council began learning, too, that key business process may need radical redesign reengineering—to generate breakthrough change in the effectiveness and efficiency of the process. The council selected an initial BPQM project to learn how to apply redesign methodology in a cross-functional team approach and to achieve process redesign results.

PILOT PROJECT SELECTION, ANALYSIS, AND LEARNING

AAL's billing and collection process was selected as the initial BPQM project. The primary goal of this effort was to redesign AAL's multiple billing systems into a single, consolidated billing and collection system for all products, offering additional payment options and increased flexibility to its payers while reducing processing costs and errors. Additional goals included developing a process redesign methodology to replicate in future BPQM efforts, and learning how to apply various analysis tools in a cross-functional project team redesign setting. Managers of the various functions within the billing and collection process were selected as team members, with objectives of redesigning the process and learning the methodology. The team enlisted the assistance of a Juran consultant to learn how to apply BPQM in process redesign.

AAL applied several analysis tools in separate phases of the billing and collection redesign project. The team began its analysis of the existing process using Juran Institute's BPQM approach to develop a detailed work flow model of the existing process, identifying process deficiencies such as re-work loops, handoffs and handbacks, and error correction activities. The team needed to understand which areas would have the biggest opportunity for improvement in a redesign effort, and chose cost of quality analysis as the tool to help determine that information. Using the detailed work flow model from the BPQM analysis, the team performed its cost of quality analysis and categorized costs as preventive, appraisal, failure and business costs. The cost of quality analysis highlighted areas of poor quality (failure costs) and areas where business costs could be reduced through process redesign. The team then used Juran Institute's BPQM approach to identify customers, research customer requirements. and develop process redesign goals.

The use of these tools provided an in-depth look at the existing process and highlighted areas to investigate in redesign efforts. However, the team needed to step away from the existing systems and procedures which had evolved over the past 20+ years, and take a fresh look at developing a new comprehensive billing and collection process. The team used information engineering (IE) methodology to examine the business process requirements. This analysis examined how data flow through the process, independent of the way processing activities are performed. This analysis resulted in detailed data and process models which applied to all products within the process. The team used this information, along with information obtained in the BPQM and COQ analyses, to develop detailed specifications from which to redesign the entire billing and collection process to meet project goals. The team completed a net present value analysis of the significant investment required to implement the redesign, and received approval for the project from the quality council. Implementation of the redesign is in progress.

One of the learnings from this initial BPQM effort is that analysis tools should be integrated to optimize cohesive information gathering. The three pieces of analysis—BPQM analysis (existing process workflow, customer requirements, redesign goals), COQ analysis, and IE analysis—were performed separately with little overlap or parallel effort. AAL decided to build its road map to integrate these tools to collect all information needed for analysis in a comprehensive, single approach, minimizing the time and effort required for data collection.

Another learning from the initial effort is that incremental improvements should be spun off into separate quality improvement efforts in order to realize some quick wins immediately. During the billing and collection process analysis, the team decided to defer acting on incremental improvement opportunities that it discovered, to see if they would be resolved in the major redesign. The team did not want to duplicate efforts required to implement incremental changes without understanding the impact on the resources needed for the redesign. In reality, there were some gains to be realized through minor information system changes coupled with changes in processing activities, and these could have been implemented in parallel with continued work on the process redesign.

DEVELOPING AAL'S ROAD MAP

Learnings from the first BPQM effort indicated there are many different ways to accomplish the goals of a BPQM project. If the characteristics of a project can be identified, the right blend of tools and techniques can be deployed. To this end, AAL developed a very simple, straightforward "road map," leveraging experiences and learnings with anticipated future needs. Although simple, this hybrid methodology is very robust. It brings together the three primary analysis disciplines at work, (BPQM, IE and COQ) along with other learnings such as techniques for building a strong team.

Essential components to any methodology are who, what, when, why and how. A methodology must be simple and pragmatic, so that people will use it. It must be replicable and adaptable to fit the goals of any effort. In other words, a team should be able to pick and choose those pieces of the methodology that make sense for the task at hand. It should support a common sense approach lending itself to *results.*

Designing a road map to integrate related tools can be risky. Some people look at such a road map as a sequenced set of instructions, with all the answers built into the design. If that were true, this would be titled "AAL's BPQM Cookbook." In reality, a road map provides suggested routes from which to choose to reach a specific destination.

The nature of redesign efforts requires the need to adjust course as goals, objectives and requirements become clearer through the data gathering activities. At each stage of the effort, the overall process needs to be continually appraised and adjusted. Ideally this adjustment is done proactively, keeping a step or two ahead of the next project step. The team may find itself reacting to discoveries which require a quick change in course, or to regulatory or technical constraints. In either case, the road map provides focus, bringing direction and some rationality to the team's process. The more it is kept in front of the team, the more everyone can feel on track and measure the team's progress.

AAL's BPQM road map was developed by integrating dimensions of project management, team dynamics, and process analysis tools with Juran Institute's BPQM training materials. Exhibit 2 (Table 5.2) illustrates the basic format of the road map. Exhibit 3 (Table 5.3) provides a detailed view of the road map AAL used in its second BPQM project, redesigning the issue and underwriting process. The rest of this paper blends concept with experience to further explain the road map.

USING THE ROAD MAP

PHASE ONE—PLANNING

Team Startup and Training

Experience from the first BPQM project proved that team selection and orientation are critical to the success of process redesign. The team must include people who are working within the process, blending managerial and front-line expertise to be able to analyze

Table 5.2 Phases, Tasks, and Steps of AAL's BPQM Road Map

AAL'S BPQM ROAD MAP COMPOSITION

Phase	Planning	Transfer to Operations	Operational Management
	Team Startup	Planning for Implementation	Ongoing Operational Management
T	Redesign Team Training	Deployment of Plan	
A	Process Definition		
S	Customer Requirements		
K	Analysis of Existing Process		
S	Process Redesign		

AAL'S BPQM ROAD MAP STRUCTURE

PHASE: Planning, Transfer to Operations

TASK: Team Startup, Process Redesign, Plan Deployment

STEP: Process Selection, Team Building

Step/Subprocess Name—"What"

Objectives—"What"

Expected Results—"What" & "Why"

Who is Involved—"Who"

Tools—"How"

Duration—"How Long" & "When"

Table 5.3 AAL's Use of BPQM Road Map for Planning Stage

PHASE I—PLANNING

Step/Subprocess	Objectives	Expected Results	Who Is Involved	Tools	Duration
A. Team Startup					
1. Process selection	Select process to redesign Select process owner Set preliminary targets for process redesign	Process, process owner identified Preliminary redesign targets set	AAL Quality Council		Pre-start
2. Team structure	Finalize team structure, roles	Team structure identified	Process owner (PO), Project team leader (PTL)		Pre-start
3. Team orientation	Introduce team members to project, timeline	Preliminary redesign targets, timeline shared with team	Redesign team (includes PO, PTL)		2 hours (12/16/94)
B. Process Redesign Team Training					
1. Team building 2. BPQM training	Team building training Tools, methodology training	Team orientation, commitment Clear roles, expectations Knowledge of tools, methodology Preliminary customer id Process boundaries High-level process flow	Redesign team Trainers	TQM, BPQM	3 days (01/18/95–01/20/95)

(Continued)

Table 5.3 (Continued)

		PHASE I—PLANNING			
Step/Subprocess	Objectives	Expected Results	Who Is Involved	Tools	Duration
C. Process Definition					
1. High level process model	Process modeling overview	Definition of existing process boundaries, scope	Redesign team	Use process decomp. & event modeling tools to record, not facilitate SISP definitions	02/01/95–03/01/95
2. Inventory existing information	Validate current process—high level model Identify process measures	Understanding of current process, expenses, cycle times			
D. Customer Requirements					
1. Customer requirements	Validate customer identification Determine customer requirements	Identified set of customers, customer requirements	Redesign team BPQM advisor (customer focus)	BPQM	03/01/95–04/01/95
E. Process Analysis					
1. Identify weaknesses, what's missing in current process	Analyze quality of current process: —identify what's missing, weaknesses in current process —assess performance against measures	Understanding of existing process Focus for process redesign: —minimize deficiencies —reduce COPQ —improve/increase process features Quick wins/solutions to be worked in line	Redesign team Ad hoc specialists for training, facilitation: —process analysis —cost of quality —quality measurement —process, data modeling —market researchers —etc.	BPQM tools COQ analysis Benchmarking tools Process analysis technique (PAT) Process decomp. & event modeling tools	03/01/95–06/01/95
2. Analyze cost of quality	—analyze cost of quality				
3. Benchmark other companies	—benchmark other companies				
4. Review team goals for redesign					

E. Process Analysis (Continued)

	Improvement opportunities to be worked in line or as QI/QP		
	Begin building gearbox (QC)		
			06/01/95–09/01/95

F. Process Redesign

		Redesign team	Out-of-the-box thinking
1. Breakthrough change concepts	Generate breakthrough process design concept(s)	Ad hoc specialists for training, facilitation:	Process decomp. & event modeling tools
2. High level business system redesign	Develop high-level business system redesign	—process analysis	Process, data modeling tools
3. Detailed process redesign	Develop detailed process redesign	—process, data modeling	Discrete event simulation tools (new)
4. Lab prototype	Build laboratory/prototype	—organizational learning	Process optimization tools (new)
5. Test, learn, iterate	Test, learn, iterate	Lab team(s)	
	End state vision of optimal process design		
	BAA outputs: process, data models, event models, data flow diagrams		
	Reactions, feedback, input from other parties		

(Continued)

Table 5.3 *(Continued)*

		PHASE 2—TRANSFER			
Step/Subprocess	Objectives	Expected Results	Who Is Involved	Tools	Duration
G. Planning for Implementation					
1. Identify implementation issue	Identify implementation issues: —staffing, training —technology —communication —etc.	Effective action plan to implement process in workable "chunks"	Redesign team Release team(s)	Business Systems Analysis, Design Best solution process Process control tools	
2. Identify process capabilities	Identify process capabilities				
3. Develop action plan for implementation	Develop action plan to implement process: —identify pilot, rollout, release —identify resources				
H. Plan Deployment					
1. Install releases toward end state vision achievement	Allocate resources for implementation Implement, learn, iterate	Resource allocation Installed releases until end state vision is achieved	Redesign team Release team(s)	Business Systems implementation	

PHASE 3—OPERATIONAL MANAGEMENT

Step/Subprocess	Objectives	Expected Results	Who Is Involved	Tools	Duration
I. Operational Management					
1. Process quality control	Implement/operate process Monitor actual process performance	Maintain control over process	Process management team	Business process quality management	Ongoing
2. Process quality improvement	Improve process	Continuous quality improvement within process	Process management team	Business process quality management	Ongoing
3. Periodic process review and assessment	Provide feedback for design/redesign decision Assess fit with other business processes, strategy	Maintain robust, responsive process	Process management team	Business process quality management	Ongoing

the existing process and identify opportunities for incremental and radical change. Selection must also include people who are outside the process, yet who support the process through their functional disciplines, such as information technology, accounting, and human resources. Some people will be identified to provide ad hoc support to the team in their areas of specific knowledge. It is important to identify these knowledge areas and the people during the planning phase, in order to keep these people "in the loop" from the beginning of the project effort, even though their support may not be needed until later. All team members must be willing and able to "wear their process hats"... to look at the process as a whole, beyond their individual roles and responsibilities within the process.

For AAL' s second BPQM effort, redesigning the issue and underwriting process, team training efforts included sharing the scope and magnitude of the process selected for redesign, teaching the methodology, and building an understanding of team dynamics. Team members were chosen from various areas and departments within and outside the process, and had not worked closely together. An objective of this training was to help team members embrace their challenge with a common focus on the task at hand and how they would work together.

By bringing the redesign and support team members together early in the effort, the team was able to maintain understanding and momentum throughout the project, even though some expertise was not requested until later steps. Downstream parties were included in many of the early sessions to observe the redesign team at work, and to begin building straw models of the process based on their areas of expertise. Then, when the team needed to see a process flow diagram or a data model, the information engineering support person was able to bring her models forward to the team for reaction and use. These support experts met separately with the team leader if they had questions or if they felt their techniques could be leveraged to help the team in its work. Thus, even though the road map suggests these activities as a later step, the support experts were visible early in the effort to hear, and participate in, discussion and decisions that shaped the goals for the project.

Process Definition and Customer Requirements

By defining the existing process boundaries where the process begins, and where it ends . . . the issue and underwriting redesign team was able to focus on the areas it needed to explore, and gave itself permission to ignore areas outside of those bounds. Developing a high-level process model provided an "inside-out" look at the existing process.

It is critical to identify the customers of the process, and to define the requirements for each of those customers. This was done through taking an "outside-in" look at the issue and underwriting process, to determine what customers expect from the results of the process.

Process Analysis

The process analysis step develops a deeper understanding of the existing process, defining the business rules the company has developed as the existing process has evolved. Here, the team walked a fine line between learning enough about today's process in order to design tomorrow's, without becoming enamored with the existing process to the point of being unable to question it.

Cost of quality analysis tools provided focus to the team. identifying areas where high failure and business costs raised suspicions about the effectiveness of the process. Once these areas were identified, the team determined where to take the analysis to a deeper level to gain a better understanding of redesign opportunities. Here, too, the team learned that some costs did not warrant further investigation, since the impact on the overall process was relatively small.

Taking the analysis to a deeper level involved performing a work-flow analysis with those people performing the processing activities. The workflow analysis identified areas of redundant activity within the process, business rules that are no longer necessary but were being followed because "we've always done it that way," and rework, handoff and handback loops that needed to be eliminated with the redesigned process. Information engineering process decomposition and data flow diagram tools modeled these findings in a way that was meaningful to process users as well as systems analysts.

It is important to obtain feedback and reaction from people within the process but outside the redesign team, to validate the team's findings in the high-level and detail-level analyses. With the issue and underwriting effort, this provided opportunities for validation and clarification before the team began its redesign work.

Use of tools such as flowcharting, formal business area analysis methodology and process analysis technique (PAT) may be helpful in this analysis. Benchmarking process costs and other measures with outside companies may provide further insights into opportunities for gaining effectiveness with process redesign.

Process Redesign

By now, the team was ready to try its hand at redesigning the process. This is where the support team members exercised their expertise in defining what they learned from the work of the redesign team. The support team prepared event, process and data models using information engineering tools, outlining interdependencies of activity within the process but independent of the way work is performed. These models reflect what must happen for the process to be effective. They enabled the redesign team to develop an efficient, effective workflow for the process with activities that add value in meeting process goals. The models also provided process specifications that are useful when designing information systems to support the redesigned process.

Again, it is critical to test the redesigned workflow by obtaining feedback and reaction from people outside the team, and to map the redesign against redesign goals. These tests provide an initial look at how well the redesign will meet customer requirements, and whether the team overlooked details which are crucial to success. These tests also may have provided an opportunity to begin communicating the degree of change to people who will be using the new process, building an understanding and commitment to successful implementation.

The redesign can be tested in iterative steps beginning with a simple explanation of the new workflow, and building to the point where computer-based discrete simulation tools can be used to prototype the redesign in a laboratory setting.

AAL's issue and underwriting BPQM team will finish the process redesign phase this fall, and will begin planning for implementation at that time.

PHASE TWO—TRANSFER TO OPERATIONS

Planning for Implementation/Deployment of Plan

It is important to focus on managing change when planning for and implementing the redesigned process. Change management includes understanding the impact of the redesign on the people performing the process and on those required to implement the change—quite often, these are the same people. Technology changes are likely, and may require different equipment and specialized training. Process measures and performance measures need revision. People will need to know what's expected of them during and after implementation.

One significant change AAL is experiencing is the use of piloting initial redesign releases with the expressed intent of learning what needs to be modified before rolling out the next implementation phase. In other words, the initial release is not expected to meet all requirements for success, but is intended to provide a taste of the redesign and an opportunity to improve—or discard—the new process. This is challenging team members and processors to collaborate on implementation and to accept ownership for delivering excellent results once the entire redesign is installed. An implementation action plan which includes phases for piloting, improving and installing subsequent releases will help everyone understand the journey to achieve the end state vision of redesign.

PHASE THREE—OPERATIONAL MANAGEMENT

Once the redesign is implemented, continuous management of the cross-functional process is needed to hold the gains and incrementally improve the operation. An ongoing process management team is assigned to monitor process performance, initiate quality improvement projects and perform a periodic review assessing the fit of this process with other strategic business processes. AAL has yet to experience this phase of the BPQM road map, but looks forward to this learning.

LEARNINGS FROM THE ROAD MAP

AAL's use of the road map for the issue and underwriting BPQM project resulted in multiple learnings, reaffirming the value of an integrated, cohesive approach to process redesign:

- The road map provided a framework within which to operate, to assess progress and to adjust course. It brought together the right people and techniques to move the effort forward and minimized the rework loop.
- The road map provided a clear, yet dynamic direction. Knowing what the next steps in the process are made it easier to gather information to be used later in the process.
- The project moved with considerable speed, maintaining momentum with clear direction and integrated data gathering.

- Team members and others involved in the effort were enthusiastic about the process, because they could feel progress toward clear goals and see results from their work sooner.
- Team members were able to work together effectively early in the process, given their training and development as a team.
- By obtaining input, feedback and involvement from front-line processors throughout the redesign process, team members felt they understood the processing requirements and were able to build a better design.
- By staying at a high level in early process definition, then using cost of quality and other analysis tools to identify where further detail was needed, team members avoided feeling bogged down in detail too early in the project.
- Involving expert analysts in the early stages of the project ensured a greater understanding redesign. The analysts kept up to speed and were able to take that understanding into their work, performed outside the team work sessions, to support the team.
- The project team leader must be able to coordinate efforts of the project team and the ad hoc efforts of the experts supporting the team's work. This is critical to keep everyone informed and on the same path.

ADAPTING THE ROAD MAP

AAL continues to learn from its road map. A forum of experts representing the three major analysis disciplines (BPQM, IE and COQ) meets periodically to monitor the progress of the second BPQM team and to address methodology issues. Members of this group agree the road map provides a valuable guideline for integrating multiple tools in a major, cross-functional redesign effort. The group is looking forward to seeing the road map improved with future BPQM projects.

Any organization can build and leverage its own road map. The basic components provide a framework for including those tools and techniques already mastered and in use at the company, or for introducing new tools. This approach permits a company to:

- Start with the road map as a guideline for bringing people and tools into a redesign effort.
- Adapt the road map to a specific BPR project, identifying tools and resources as part of the project planning, and adjusting the road map during the course of the project.
- Use the road map to assess the progress of the project, and to guide the team through data-gathering activities in a comprehensive way.
- Learn from initial BPR efforts, and enhance the road map as the level of sophistication within the company increases or as new tools and techniques are factored into the process.

The beauty of any road map is that it provides alternatives to consider in planning a journey. AAL's advice to any company considering such an integrated approach:

1. PICK THE "SENSIBLE" ROUTE!
2. PLAN FOR A FEW "DETOURS"!

Self-Directed Work Teams

Some managers have accused quality advocates of wanting to establish elaborate "bureaucracies" and force both managers and employees to use rigid procedures to solve problems. In fact, a cardinal principle of managing for quality is that opportunities for improving performance should be identified and implemented at the lowest level of the organization capable of identifying and addressing them. Designing and implementing the infrastructure—e.g., Education and Training, described in Chapter 4—enables both individuals and teams to assume additional responsibilities. Middle and senior managers are then free to define, focus, and facilitate the changes that are required to continuously enhance their organizations' performance. An evolving approach to simultaneous enhancement of employee satisfaction and performance is the use of self-directed work teams. The following example, presented by Droege et al. (1993), provides valuable insights to the lessons learned from piloting and implementing self-directed work teams within a multifunctional services department at Caterpillar:

BACKGROUND

Caterpillar's total employment is approximately 50,000. This story is about 170 employees and their journey toward becoming self-directed work teams and empowered people. The employees are located in Peoria and East Peoria, Illinois. They belong to a department that consists of three divisions: Purchasing, Administration and Travel, and Traffic & Indirect Materials. We provide a variety of corporate services, such as: central purchasing, warehousing, and distribution of indirect materials (products/services consumed in support of the manufacturing and assembly of our products); negotiations with and development of major carriers for transportation by air, land, or water; coordination of domestic and international household moves; negotiations with vehicle leasing companies and airlines for Caterpillar travel; management of the corporate aircraft and hangar facility located at the Greater Peoria Airport; etc. Eighty percent of the people in our department work in an office environment, with the other 20% involved with warehousing or interplant transportation (automotive/diesel repair).

PROBLEM DEFINITION

Caterpillar began to decentralize, creating profit and service centers. Our department belongs to one of the service centers. The purpose of our existence is to provide support to our internal customers which includes both profit centers and other service centers. If we couldn't meet or exceed the value provided by an outside supplier, we risked losing the business. We were no longer the "only game in town." Our department was meeting and, in some cases, exceeding our objectives for 1989 but our internal customers wanted more. They expected "outstanding" results with no exception. Most discussions with customers focused on two key issues: decreased cost and improved responsiveness. To be successful in meeting customer needs, some within our department knew we needed to change our way of doing business.

DISCOVERY

Through visits to other companies, some of our managers had discovered that self-directed teams were successfully addressing challenges similar to ours. The teams were not always called self-directed. Some were called self-managing teams, autonomous teams, project teams, quality circles, semi-autonomous teams, etc. The teams we were interested in had a common characteristic, in that they were empowered to make decisions rather than just make recommendations about projects or day-to-day work.

Numerous success stories were found in a variety of publications:

- General Mills: A 40% increase in productivity.
- Aid Association for Lutherans: 20% increase in productivity.
- Carrier: Reduced unit turnaround from 2 weeks to 2 days.
- A.O. Smith: Manager/worker ratio from 1/10 to 1/34.
- Federal Express: Service errors reduced by 13%.
- 3M Corporation: Tripled in number of new products.
- Johnsonville Foods: 50% increase in productivity.
- Dana Corporation: Reduced 6-month lead time to 6 weeks.
- Volvo Corporation: Reduced defects by 90%.

These were the types of results our internal customers wanted. We knew when we started that it meant a culture shock for our organization. Aware of both the potential impact and the potential benefits of pursuing this change, our director and department manager initiated the change process by planting the idea with several individuals in our department. They continued to show interest and, after a period of time, others became interested. Information about empowered teams* from magazines, books, newspapers, etc., began moving up and down the department, along with a cross section of people visiting other companies.

REMEDIAL JOURNEY

In 1989, our department manager decided to "test the water" to see if one of our work groups wanted to pilot self-direction. He, with help from others, prepared a rough vision of what the future could be with self-directed teams and met with an entire division to share this vision. At the end of the meeting, he asked if one of the work groups present would volunteer as a pilot team for self-direction. A lone hand was raised and our journey officially began.

The pilot team began by working with their advisor† to determine which decisions they would make versus ones their advisor would make. Easy decisions were addressed first. Almost concurrent with their work on decision making, they worked on team design by flow-charting team processes and determining changes in design for process improvements. Problem solving techniques that were taught in the '80s and used by a variety of Juran teams and Annual Quality Improvement teams to address specific projects were now being applied daily to address a broad range of problems. Not all members on the pilot team were equally excited about the additional new responsibilities being undertaken. Our pilot team went through the typical development stages of forming, storming, norming, and performing. In fact, enough storming existed after six months that we were questioning whether we wanted to continue. But continue we did, and for the next four

---

* The term "Empowered Team" is used interchangeably with "Self-directed Team."
† "Advisor" is our term for a past supervisor or manager.

months the pilot team started moving through the norming and performing phases with results that definitely rated "exceptional."

Some of the results achieved by the pilot team during the first year were:

- Went from having 2 buyers to 1 buyer.
- 4–5 days' Purchase Order process time reduced to 1.
- 5 Inventory Analysts reduced to 4.
- Autocratic assignments turned into team-given challenges.
- Internal conflict was addressed by the team.
- 2 Records Clerks reduced to 1.
- Vacation time, personal time, absences managed by the pilot team.

Because of the pilot's success, our department manager encouraged the remaining work groups to start the journey toward becoming self-directed. We had a variety of responses from our teams. Some were reluctant; however, since the department manager had requested it, for many that was the equivalent of a directive. We knew from the variety of opinions at the beginning that the rate of progress toward self-direction would vary from team to team due to the level of buy-in by each team member.

Most information gathered about this change pointed to management as being the major obstacle to empowerment but at the same time having a major role during implementation. Simply put, management has "power" that needs to be transferred to the teams, and the change doesn't start until this transfer begins. Support for the change varied among our advisors. Managers played different roles. Our department manager acted very much like a pilot trying to keep us on course; some advisors acted as navigators to help track and guide the process; some acted as passengers, just going along for the ride; and, of course, some advisors were manning the artillery and started taking shots. Some of the passengers, and particularly the gunners, figured this was just the "flavor of the month." After all, we were the only ones crazy enough to try this at Caterpillar! If we play along, this change will eventually die a deserved death. WRONG! We knew we needed to increase buy-in at the management level, just as we needed to do with the front line.

Our way of doing this was to get advisors involved in facilitating the change. We had a small team of AQI (Annual Quality Improvement) coordinators consisting of only advisors from the three divisions within our department when the pilot team started. This team gradually grew to 12 management members representing the three divisions of self-directed teams. Eventually, membership included all levels (cross section) with five focus teams. In the early stages, this team met once a month with the department manager acting as facilitator. They tracked the progress of the change and addressed any obstacles to self-direction. Its early name was the Departmental Coordinating Team until our teams indicated that "coordinating" hinted at "direction." So we've changed its name to the Departmental Support Team (DST). The role and organization of this team has changed several times during our journey and continues to change based on input from our teams and others. The DST is not a design team. As stated earlier, each team is responsible and accountable for its own design.

From all the information gathered, it was apparent that there would be fewer advisors as changes progressed. They made it to their current position because of their expertise, know-how and drive, plus they enjoyed the authority and prestige it brought. All of this was being threatened because of this new direction. The department manager realized that he would have to "walk the talk," thereby setting the example for the other advisors and yet providing a high degree of pressure on others to begin traveling down the road to empowerment. Direction was more in the form of wishes or "What I'd like to see" or "What I think we should do" or "Why not do this?" The old method of management served us well in that wishes and desires were many times interpreted as direction.

In general, our advisors have had and still have an extremely challenging and difficult journey. They continue to move from decision makers and rule enforcers to facilitators of front-line people throughout the change process. More of their time becomes devoted to removing barriers across functions and eliminating excessive procedures. A major effort for some *is to "stop killing the messenger" and to learn that this change is driven by the belief that there are no limits on the abilities or contributions derived from a properly selected, trained, supported, committed, and involved group of people. It has required a new openness by our advisors toward new ideas, new concepts, and above all their support in reinforcing and rewarding positive new behaviors.*

During 1991, the Departmental Support Team began discussing the development needs for our movement toward self-directed teams. Using brainstorming and prioritization techniques, we determined 10 areas that we needed to focus on for future growth. We called each area a building block, fully realizing that we needed to form these blocks into a foundation of support for this change. Our 10 building blocks are:

1. Executive commitment.

2. Vision.

3. Trust.

4. Freedom to fail and try again.

5. Time.

6. Training.

7. Transition plan.

8. Incentive.

9. Anticipation and management of diversity.

10. Obsession to exceed customer expectations.

Please understand that one doesn't necessarily come before another, except for the first two listed. A management commitment and a vision of how things will change are essential to effectively starting the change process. The blocks are continuously being addressed during the transition years and are changed as required.

Over the next several pages, we will discuss the building blocks in more detail.

EXECUTIVE COMMITMENT

This is a key building block at the start and during the process. When commitment starts in the middle of the organization as it did with our change, it needs to be promoted to increase support and commitment at upper levels. As it is accepted and believed that top management is supportive of the change, people begin to change.

Commitment for our change started at our department manager level. He kept the change alive by promoting the concept of empowered people and teams at all levels in the organization. He was willing to talk about self-directed teams to anyone wanting to listen and even to those who did not want to listen. He realized that a change of this nature, to be sustained, would have to have increased buy-in both inside and outside our department. About 18 months into the process, he placed an advisor on staff assignment with responsibility for facilitating the development and promotion of the empowerment process internally and externally. He also acted as team leader for the Departmental Support Team. As more people began hearing the success stories, increased buy-in led to increased support and commitment up and down the organization. From a kernel of commitment within the organization, we are witnessing today a growth in commitment throughout Caterpillar. In July 1991, our movement toward empowered people and teams received a boost when Don Fites, Chairman and Chief Executive Officer, made the following comment in a Caterpillar management newsletter.

"I believe we're accomplishing what we set out to do.... We're pushing accountability and responsibility for results down into the organization...and we're empowering people to get the job done."

VISION

Our vision, as discussed earlier, started as a list of statements describing what the future could look like if we implemented self-directed teams. The Departmental Support Team used this set of statements to establish the following long-range vision:

"By empowering people and teams, we expect to bring a new vitality to the workplace by tapping into human creativity and innovation."

We determined a number of missions tied to this vision and categorized them into three major areas: Improvement of measurable outputs; development of people, and greater organizational effectiveness.

For improving measurable outputs, we targeted improved customer satisfaction and employee satisfaction, fully believing the two are inseparable. Service and product quality, delivery and timeliness, and cost effectiveness are all targets of continuous improvement for our teams. They use a tool to track measurable performance that we call a scoreboard (see Figure 5.10). Team objectives are listed down the left side, and progress is monitored monthly by the teams.

The continuous development of people is an exciting mission. Through cross training and classroom instruction, people began to increase their skill and knowledge levels, providing greater flexibility and higher levels of self-esteem and commitment. A typical comment from our front lines after a year into this change was that they now had an opportunity to use their brains at work rather than turning them off when they arrive at work and back on when they leave. People taking college business courses in hopes of eventual advancement now had the opportunity to apply theory to real business problems addressed by their team.

Organizational effectiveness began as teams started assuming decision-making responsibilities once performed by front-line or mid-level advisors. This has resulted in fewer advisors and fewer levels which, in turn, leads to reduced cost, more innovation/creativity from the front line, and quicker response to the customer.

1993 SCOREBOARD													
	Obj	Jan	Feb	Mar	Apr	May	Jun	Jul	Aug	Sep	Oct	Nov	Dec
QUALITY													
System grief	3%												
NN receipts	95%												
PCD grief	7%												
Certified suppliers	42												
COST													
Exp. budget (5.8M)	6.1M												
Net price changes	.05%												
One time decreases	4.5M												
ASSETS													
Add. EDI suppliers	32												
ZWIP delivery %	96%												
Inventory turns	9.0												
Parts past due	5%												
Inventory $	5%												
PEOPLE													
Customer visits	250												
Education and training	2 Per												

Figure 5.10 Caterpillar Self-Directed Team Scoreboard.

TRUST

Trust is earned. It takes a long time to build and only a few seconds to destroy! It holds team members together and it keeps them moving toward self-direction. It means managers have to "walk the talk." It means team members' having confidence in each other's abilities and a genuine concern for team success. It is a binding force not only within the team but also throughout the organization. A wrong word, a decision made without team input, a team decision reversed, a member perceived as not doing his/her share, a member more concerned with "I" than "we" can hinder the bonding that needs to take place between team members as well as up and down the organization.

As trust grows, treasure and protect it. Whether a team member or an advisor, remember, your actions speak louder than your words!

FREEDOM TO FAIL AND TRY AGAIN

Even with the best of training, teams make mistakes! Expect it and accept it as part of the learning/growing process similar to what individuals go through when learning a new job.

When mistakes are made, advisors need to allow the team to correct its own mistakes while providing whatever support it may need. Correcting a mistake for a team results in a missed opportunity for furthering team development and a resistance from the team toward future decision making.

TIME

Participation and facilitation of the change process pose a significant strain on time, due to the classroom training, cross training, and team development stages (form, storm, norm, & perform). Team members also join departmental support teams to discuss and solve a variety of challenges during implementation. Each building block has been created through input from several people and teams in our department and is refined as we move along our journey.

Effective change occurs as all 10 building blocks are formed and refined through a high level of employee involvement. Omission of any can have a significant impact on the rate of change. It was and still is challenging for us to find the time to address the refinement of these building blocks as the change continues. We know that support and commitment would wane during the early stages if time were not devoted to promotion. Without time to create and maintain vision, confusion results. If time for training is not provided, expect a high level of anxiety due to people wanting to do the job but not having the know-how. If the advisor and team fail to take the time to plan and document a transition plan, a lot of false starts can be expected. Each area needs to be continually addressed with the highest possible level of people involvement without sacrificing customer satisfaction.

It isn't easy. In our situation, we estimate it will take four to six years to reach the vision we started with.

We established a training team with representatives from each division within our department. This team worked with the Caterpillar Training Institute and the Caterpillar Human Resource center to determine the skills and training required for self-directed teams. We found that three categories of skills needed to be addressed: interpersonal and communication, technical, and business. Technical skills were generally in place since our teams were established around natural work groups and generally had a strong technical background. Business skills would be needed, but who better to teach business skills than the advisor who had been managing the business for years? The training team determined we needed to focus on improving interpersonal and communication skills. They developed what are now known as the "core" classes for our department. Normally, classes taught in our building have people attending from a variety of areas. We elected to have classes for just the people in our department. We tried to get a good cross section of people signed up for each class. By doing this, they were not only learning new skills but also getting to know one another and share feelings about the change process.

From our list of core courses, team members are asked to take three courses focusing on how teams operate, how personality styles vary, and how to empower yourself. Team leaders are asked to take an additional course on how to lead meetings, handle conflict, etc. Advisors take a fifth course on how to empower others and nurture empowerment.

The core courses were established to get us started. People in our department attend two to three training sessions per year, well beyond the recommended core classes. During our journey, training decisions have been transferred to the teams, with the training team now acting as a resource when teams cannot find training for specific skills.

We believe that if you have well-informed, well-trained employees with the authority to make the necessary decisions to serve customers, you will have an efficient, content workforce with an obsession to exceed customer expectations.

TRANSITION PLAN

We had no formal transition plan for the first 18 months. Although we had communicated, many teams and advisors had elected to informally decide on who would make what decisions. In early 1991, teams were becoming frustrated because advisors were reversing decisions made by the team, and advisors were becoming frustrated because teams were making decisions that the advisors thought were inappropriate. We were experiencing several false starts into self-direction. We solved the problem through a series of brainstorming sessions to determine what decisions teams would make and what decisions management would make. Team decisions were placed into three categories: those requiring little or no training, those requiring training, and those requiring a high degree of training.

A transition plan (see Figure 5.11) or a left hand/right hand chart, as many refer to it in our department, resulted from the brainstorming sessions. When we started, all decisions were on the left-hand side of the chart. The chart shows what the shift of responsibilities should be and the degree of training involved before doing so. Teams and advisors review this document periodically to determine their degree of transition (movement from left to right). Then teams, along with their advisors, decide on when they want to assume responsibility for additional decisions and work with their advisors to get the necessary training.

MANAGEMENT

TEAM

- ADMINISTER SALARIES, CLASSIFICATIONS, & PERSONNEL PRACTICES
- ESTABLISH DIVISIONAL/ DEPARTMENT VISION/OBJECTIVES
- EVALUATE & PROVIDE FEEDBACK
- PERFORM AS TRAINER/LEADER/ ADVISOR

TRANSITION

TRANSFERRED PER TEAM WITH LITTLE OR NO TRAINING:

- DECIDE ON WORK DISTRIBUTION AND RESPONSIBILITIES
- ESTABLISH WORK SCHEDULE TIME, VACATIONS, AND PERSONAL TIME
- DETERMINE EQUIPMENT NEEDS AND SUPPLIES
- WORK AREA ARRANGEMENT AND EVIRONMENT
- ESTABLISH TEAM PRIORITIES
- DETERMINE TEAM MEMBERSHIP
- CROSS-TRAIN WITHIN CELL
- SELECT LEADERSHIP
- DECIDE ON CUSTOMER AND SUPPLIER TRAVEL
- DEVELOP CELL MEASUREMENTS
- PROVIDE INPUT FOR TEAM MEMBER REPLACEMENTS
- DETERMINE EDUCATION AND TRAINING NEEDS
- DETERMINE RECOGNITION AND REWARD FOR EXCEPTIONAL PERFORMANCE

TRANSFERRED PER TEAM AFTER TRAINING:

- SETS OBJECTIVES AND SCOREBOARD (CELL MEASUREMENTS)
- PREPARE AND CONDUCT TEAM FOCUSED PRESENTATIONS
- SET PRIORITIES FOR SERVICE AND ADVISORY GROUPS
- DETERMINE CUSTOMER NEEDS AND MEASUREMENT TECHNIQUE FOR CUSTOMER SATISFACTION
- ARBITRATE TEAM MEMBER CONFLICTS
- EVALUATE ADVISOR
- DETERMINE QUALITY/CERTIFICATION GOALS

TRANSFERRED PER TEAM AFTER A HIGH DEGREE OF TRAINING:

- PREPARE BUSINESS PLAN
- EVALUATE TEAM PERFORMANCE
- DEVELOP TEAM BUDGET (EXPENSES–LABOR)
- EVALUATE TEAM MEMBERS PERFORMANCE
- DEVELOP TEAM GUIDELINES FOR INITIAL DISCIPLINARY MEASURES

PLANNED JOURNEY

4 to 6 Years

ONE STEP FORWARD ONE STEP BACK

Figure 5.11 Transition Planning for Caterpillar's Self-Directed Teams.

All 16 teams are at different stages of transition. Teams have to mature and people have to become comfortable and knowledgeable about their new decision-making abilities. The rate of transition is different for each team. As teams begin to address tougher issues, such as the handling of internal conflict, peer evaluations, work effort, people reductions, etc., the rate of transition slows.

INCENTIVE

An analogy frequently used is that incentive is like the accelerator in a car. The more you push it, the faster you go. On the plus side, empowering people and teams tends to have some natural accelerators.

Most people on the front line desire more input into how they do their jobs and the business decisions affecting their team, division, and department. They like to be listened to and want their opinions requested and respected. As they become empowered, they tend to want more.

Advisors begin to see locked-up potential released from others as they move to roles of facilitation versus that of decision maker. As they witness the results and positive changes in people and teams, they have a natural tendency to increase empowerment.

Recognition and rewards are naturally used for providing incentive. One of our project teams determined, by canvassing our teams, that ideal recognition and rewards are not always monetary. Recognition can take many forms. A "thank you," an "Atta boy," a simple certificate of accomplishment or a note complimenting someone on a job well done, verbal recognition in front of the team, etc., are powerful tools for providing incentive and building enthusiasm and confidence. Advisors are encouraged to make a real effort to catch people in the act of doing the right things.

ANTICIPATION AND MANAGEMENT OF DIVERSITY

One way to silence any diversity is simply to "kill the messengers." Even after three-plus years, we still have some who practice this technique of control, knowingly or unknowingly. For the most part, our advisors are beginning to appreciate and value the variety of input from team members and openly encourage team members to express their opinions. And what a variety of opinions!

Advisors are learning to walk a "tightrope." They realize management must still make some decisions. When decisions are being considered that impact the work our people do, they are learning to seek input from those affected before making a final decision. They also tend to share the logic behind any such decision with those affected by it. For some, it's not an easy thing to do.

We gained a perspective on the diversity within our department during March 1992. We wanted a way to measure our progress toward empowering people and teams, so we utilized a survey that has 14 statements about empowerment. Our people were asked to indicate whether they strongly agree, agree, disagree, or strongly disagree with each statement. Agreement with all the statements indicates a high level of empowerment.

The results of the survey (Figure 5.12) show the diversity within our department.

Each statement shows a difference of opinion that must be addressed in order to move forward. As an example, for statement 9, some think their team has all the skills required, others think not. For statement 3, some think the advisors support empowerment

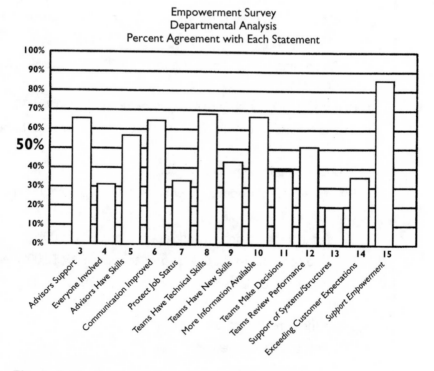

Figure 5.12 Results of Surveying Caterpillar Self-Directed Teams.

and others think not. After conducting this survey, a project team was established for any statement having less than 50% agreement. This approach resulted in improvement in almost all areas when we conducted our September (1992) survey. We were especially delighted with the fact that 85%+ of the people taking the survey expressed support for the journey toward empowered people teams. If this survey had been available when we started, we estimate that overall support was probably less than 30%.

OBSESSION TO EXCEED CUSTOMER EXPECTATIONS

Most importantly, don't lose sight of the customer, the overriding reason for implementation.

Periodically, we ask teams to submit two results attributable to the change. Most of our teams could fill a book. Below is but a sample of results recently submitted that positively impact our customers.

- Reducing and Streamlining Reports: $11,380 + accuracy improved 40%.
- Reduced paper handling resulting in reduced cost: $198,000.
- Created Requisition Tracking Report to improve customer response.
- Reduced inventory by $5,600,000.
- Established a Seal Room Segment & Ring Consignment Program.
- Consolidated 10 suppliers into an integrated source.
- Revised a purchase order routing procedure: $540,000.
- Reduced costs of distributing IE specs to supplier by $8,000/year.
- Eliminated redundant tooling system (STC): $141,333/year savings.
- Established credit card program with suppliers.
- 40% improvement in report accuracy.

Improved measurable outputs in customer and employee satisfaction, service and product quality, delivery and timeliness, and cost effectiveness are being recognized more and more as our teams mature. These results continually lend support to the reason we chose to remain with empowered work teams and people. We recognize the decision to begin was, and remains, a sound one.

THINGS TO REMEMBER

If, after reading our story, you decide to take this journey toward phenomenal results, here is a list things for you to remember:

- Promote benefits of the change.
- Form and continually refine your building blocks.
- Remember, teams are not self-directed in the beginning.
- Understand that teams are not designed the same nor will they progress at the exact same pace.
- "Buy in" is evolutionary rather than revolutionary.
- It takes time and a lot of it.
- Teams have to be allowed to grow, and people need to feel secure.
- It's not always a straight upward path. There will be periods when teams will slide backward.
- Allow teams the freedom to fail and try again.
- Don't kill the messengers.
- Develop the necessary skills whether they be technical, business, or interpersonal and communication.
- Managers must learn to take one step back for each step the team moves forward (formulate a transition plan).
- Start with easy decisions and work toward the tougher ones.

CONCLUSION

We are a customer, team-driven organization. We believe in what we are doing. Because of our implementation of self-directed teams, we expect to not only satisfy our customers, but delight them by

> meeting all their expectations in a timely manner to become our customers' "provider of choice." We know that this is possible for others willing to accept the challenge, begin the journey, and make the sacrifices encountered. We think we have completed approximately 70% of our journey. It's an exciting, demanding journey and one that completely changed the way we do things from the bottom to the top of our organization. It's not easy. The 170 people in our department make it work. Without their perseverance, patience, belief, faith, and trust in what we hoped to achieve, this change would never have become a reality.
>
> This is the epitome of participative management. Work life will never be the same.

Expanding the Scope of Measurements

Concurrently with the expansion of the dimensions of organizational coverage and types of teams, the scope and types of performance measures are enlarged. For example, as the use of Quality Planning teams is expanded, they, as part of Juran's Quality Planning Road Map, are required to develop measures and goals for:

1. Customer (internal/external) satisfaction for the products of their planning projects.

2. Product features' performance, e.g., reliability and courtesy.

3. Process features' performance, e.g., process capability.

4. Process controls, e.g., upper and lower control limits for process control charts.

Furthermore, benchmarking (competitive and best practices) and Quality Assessments are being used to help establish strategic and derivative operational goals for the organization's product

Figure 5.13 Drivers for Measures Resulting from Expanding the Quality System.

and processes.* The introduction of Business Process Management requires the development of measures for processes' effectiveness and efficiency.† Similarly, initiating Quality for Work Groups necessitates the development of measures for departmental processes. And finally, measures and goals for individuals have to be aligned with the goals for their work units, departments, divisions, and the total organization.

Now that we have discussed each of the dimensions of expansion, the construct presented as Figure 1.7 can be better appreciated and is therefore reproduced here as Figure 5.13.

---

* Stodd et al. (1996) at Kaiser Permanente reported on the approach and results of a benchmarking team's study of Operating Room (OR) Utilization that identified best practices which, if implemented across all of Kaiser's Main OR's would result in $72.6 million in savings which included $21.7 million in potential savings from OR materials. To ensure that the benchmarking project's results were used to drive future improvements, the potential savings were then "included in organizational budgeting projections."
† Measures of effectiveness are focused on determining the extent to which customers' needs have been met. Measures of efficiency are focused on determining if the customers' needs have been met with minimal cost to the organization.

Expand Phase: Roles and Responsibilities of Upper Managers

Figure 5.14 is a checklist of "deeds to be done" by upper managers in the Expand Phase. Note that, in the context of expanding the quality system infrastructure, as well as in the number and type of project teams, the word "mandate" is used. At this stage of an organization's quality initiative, both upper and middle managers should have completed the tasks required to place their organizational units in a state of "self-control." This implies that both the current and new units know what they are expected to do, have the resources to do it, are provided with accurate and timely feedback on how well they are performing, and finally, are

Decide	Prepare	Start	**Expand**	Integrate

Tasks for Upper Managers

- Support quality infrastructure.
- Support expansion of teams.
- Participate in training.
- Participate in projects.
- Mandate quality improvement.
- Mandate quality planning.
- Mandate expansion of quality control.
- Identify key business processes.
- Create key business process teams.
- Identify benchmarking opportunities.

Figure 5.14 An Expand Phase Checklist for Upper Managers.

recognized and rewarded for exemplary performance with respect to leading and managing for quality.

HIGHLIGHTS OF CHAPTER 5

1. The Expand Phase is comprised of activities that simultaneously enlarge the scope of the organization's quality initiative in multiple dimensions:

    a. The number of organizational units participating.

    b. The number of teams that are active and productive.

    c. The types of project teams that are being trained and employed.

    d. The types of measures used to prioritize the projects on which the teams are focused.

    Within the new organizational units, the infrastructure developed in the Start Phase should be replicated and used to drive and support their pilot project initiatives.

2. *Quality planning* teams using Juran's Quality Planning Road Map can significantly increase the effectiveness of both operations and administrative products and processes.

3. At the departmental level, quality control and improvement are implemented by using the *Quality for Work Groups Process*.

4. Business Process Quality Management (BPQM) teams can be used to identify, control, and improve (including reengineering) an organization's key business processes.

5. Self-directed work teams provide significant opportunities for simultaneous cost reduction, performance improvement, and improvement in employee job satisfaction. However, transition planning is critical for their successful implementation.

6. Cascading and systematically expanding the organization's quality system results in an aligned set of performance measures.

References

Braid, J. (1988). "Catalyst for a New Culture: Getting Employees Involved in Quality," *Proceedings Juran Institute's IMPRO Conference,* Juran Institute, Wilton, CT.

Brennan, J. (1991). "Investing in Quality at the Vanguard Group: If It's Not Broken, Improve it Anyway," *Proceedings Juran Institute's IMPRO Conference,* Juran Institute, Wilton, CT.

Droege, R., Tolbert, L., and Rutledge, J. (1993). "Changing the Organization from Within: Self-Directed Work Teams in a Service Function," *Proceedings Juran Institute's IMPRO Conference,* Juran Institute, Wilton, CT.

Hooyman, J., and Lane, R. (1995). "AAL's BPQM Road Map, Integrating Process Analysis Techniques," *Proceedings Juran Institute's IMPRO Conference,* Juran Institute, Wilton, CT.

Joines, R. (1994). "Eastman's Quality Journey and Lessons Learned: A Baldrige Award Winner's Case Study," *Proceedings Juran Institute's IMPRO Conference,* Juran Institute, Wilton, CT.

Juran, J. (Editor-in Chief). (1995). A *History of Managing for Quality,* Quality Press, Milwaukee, WI.

Juan, J. (1992). *Juran on Quality by Design* (Free Press, New York, NY).

Mason, M., and Long, T. (1992). "Stanford University Hospital: Organizing for Quality Planning & Undertaking the Cost Accounting QP Process," *Proceedings Juran Institute's IMPRO Conference,* Juran Institute, Wilton, CT.

Morse, W.R. (1996). "Reengineering of the Field Representative Recruiting and Selecting System," *Proceedings Juran Institute's IMPRO Conference,* Juran Institute, Wilton, CT.

Quality for Work Groups, Facilitator's Guide. (1992). Juran Institute, Wilton, CT.

Re-Engineering Processes for Competitive Advantage (Business Process Quality Management). (1994). Juran Institute, Wilton, CT.

Satterthwaite, F. (1995). "The Vanguard Quality Partnership," *Proceedings Juran Institute's IMPRO Conference,* Juran Institute, Wilton, CT.

Stodd, K., Ortiz, A., and Tenzer, I. (1996). "Operating Room Benchmarking Study: The Kaiser Experience," *Proceedings Juran Institute's IMPRO Conference,* Juran Institute, Wilton, CT.

Stratton, D. (1992). "Excellence Through Quality—A Quality Improvement Process That Works," *Proceedings Juran Institute's IMPRO Conference,* Juran Institute, Wilton, CT.

Walden, J. (1986). "Integrating Customer Satisfaction into Daily Work," *Proceedings Juran Institute's IMPRO Conference,* Juran Institute, Wilton, CT.

Young, J. (1990). "Enabling Quality Improvement in British Telecom," *Proceedings Juran Institute's IMPRO Conference,* Juran Institute, Wilton, CT.

CHAPTER 6

Integration: Perpetuating Performance Improvement

Ironically, during a consulting assignment at a snow-surrounded hospital in North Dakota, the author was introduced to the term "Golden Wave." The hospital had been on the receiving end of multiple performance-improvement programs that had crested and dissipated like "Golden Waves" on the hard shore of health-care reality. This chapter focuses on the concepts and processes required to avoid the "Golden Wave" syndrome. Organizations that have implemented these processes report that they have resulted in accelerating and perpetuating performance improvement. In fact, although their planning processes' initial focus may have been restricted to quality, they have successfully expanded their scope to define, lead, and manage all dimensions of organizational performance.

Defining Factors for the Integrate Phase

The implementation of the quality system infrastructure discussed and exemplified in the Start Phase and the Expand Phase establishes four key factors that can be used as a basis for driving the integration of quality into the "lifelines" of any organization:

1. Establishing *organizational-level stretch goals* for all dimensions of performance.

2. Identifying and managing the key *business processes and goals* required to implement the organization's strategy for performance improvement.

3. Designing *jobs and people's goals* to support key departmental processes.

4. Conducting regular *reviews and audits* of actual performance at the organizational, system, process, and job performer levels.

Figure 6.1 depicts the desired interrelationships among these factors for both driving and perpetuating performance improvement.

The macrolevel approach for leading and managing key business processes was discussed in the Expand Phase (Chapter 5). This chapter will provide examples of how world-class organizations have aligned their goals with the goals for their key business processes, departments, and jobs within the departments. The examples will also demonstrate how organizations regularly review their progress against the resultant hierarchy of goals.

The lack of an integrative approach to defining and aligning corporate priorities can be manifested by either a "Random Acts of Improvement Syndrome" or team failures followed by organization

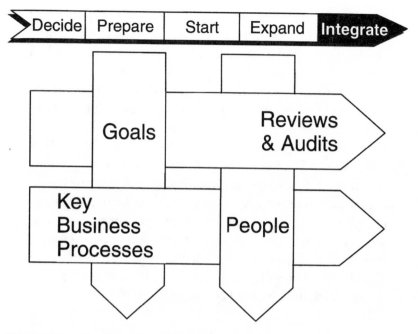

Figure 6.1 Key Factors for Quality System Perpetuation.

frustration. Reporting from their experience at US WEST, Young and Lorentz (1993) stated:

Problem-solving teams were formed around customer problems but there was often little direction from sponsors and no structure to help the team along with their work. Teams attempted to work on huge problems that had existed within the company for years. Facilitators had little experience with the process, and progress was slow. Often the team would make recommendations to sponsors who rejected the team solutions. There was no process to align efforts across organizations on the vital few problems that would increase customer satisfaction. . . . [A] quality assessment by Juran Institute consultants found strengths in our employee commitment to quality. Employee commitment was strong at all levels. They found employees performed in spite of organizational and managerial changes constantly going on around them. Employees were found to be genuinely excited when they had an opportunity to improve quality. Weaknesses found by the assessment were the lack of communicated corporate priorities; corporate business processes not managed cross-functionally, and an ineffective quality process infrastructure. There were no specific performance indicators focused on the needs of the customer. Because of the lack of cross-functional or cross-organization focus, upstream process control and prevention of problems were not widely practiced. Conflicting incentives existed in some cases that led to internal competition and suboptimization across organizations. . . . The assessment confirmed that the problems with quality improvement at U S WEST were not with employees, but with the management systems, including internal communications.

Goal Definition, Deployment, and Management

A key process for identifying, defining, communicating, and aligning strategic goals throughout the organization is "policy deployment."* Figure 6.2 provides a macrolevel view of the policy deployment process.†

---

* In an attempt to avoid confusion that results from the translation of the Japanese term, *Hoshin Kanri,* with the more common usage of the word *"policy,"* Juran (1989) has used the term *"goal* deployment."

† In the Integrate Phase, the scope of policy deployment contains multiple dimensions of organizational performance, e.g. quality, cost, profitability, safety, etc. E.G. Whitaker (1993), at Eastman Chemical, stated: "Initially we attempted to deal with quality (plans) separately from other strategic planning functions such as business plans, capital plans, and human resource plans. Incorporating all elements into one comprehensive plan was a vital step in the development of the process we now use."

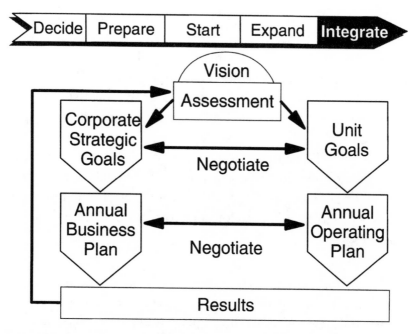

Figure 6.2 Macro-Level View of Policy Deployment Process.

The purpose of Figure 6.2 is to demonstrate that high-performance organizations' strategic goals result from:

1. Assessing (via SWOT, situational analysis, benchmarking, quality assessments) the organization's overall status versus its vision and mission.

2. Defining the "vital few" gaps, and developing strategic goals that, if met, will drive performance improvements.

3. Negotiating supporting goals with the business units.

4. Identifying, via business planning, the projects and resources needed to attain the goals.

5. Periodically comparing actual versus planned progress, and defining the necessary changes to the original projects and the business strategy.

A key concept is that the policy deployment process results in either programs (with multiple projects, e.g., new product lines or research portfolios) or individual projects. In either case, the resultant projects can be classified via Juran's Trilogy. Project milestones should then be established for each phase/step of the particular project-type's road map—e.g., planning, control, or improvement.

At U S WEST, Young and Lorentz (1993) discussed how, in response to Juran Institute's diagnosis of the lack of alignment and support of its corporate priorities with projects and resources, U S WEST used policy deployment to focus on its key business processes:

The first reaction [to Juran Institute's conclusions from its assessment] was to develop a TQM System that would support and integrate corporate direction with improvement efforts, provide for cross-functional quality efforts, and improve communication and involvement of employees. . . . Policy Management is the process led by upper management to focus the company on a few high-priority issues. One of the tools used in Policy Management is Voice of the Customer. This tool takes actual customer information and, through a systematic approach, links customer needs to business processes. This linkage helps leadership focus on the vital few activities that will achieve breakthrough improvement. Other objectives of Policy Management are to improve communication and attain broad participation in the achievement of goals. . . . Objectives of Policy Management are to assure the development of long- and short-term plans to achieve the U S WEST vision. This includes the development of indicators or measures for the plans, and the linkage of all activities to the indicators, beginning with top management and concluding with line employees. . . . Corporate measures were established from the [strategic and tactical] plans that would focus corporate

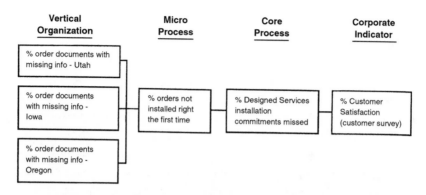

Figure 6.3 Deploying and Aligning Indicators for Customer Satisfaction and Key Business Processes at U S WEST.

resources on improving product and service availability and reliability, customer service quality and perceived value by customers, reducing costs of doing business, increasing revenue and profit, market share, and reducing new product development cycle time. . . . indicators or measures were cascaded throughout the organization to all process levels. This "flag" system of indicators connects efforts across processes and organizations. The indicators are easy for employees to understand and they can be applied at high and low levels of the company. An example of the "flag" approach used for aligning indicators associated with customer satisfaction is shown (Figure 6.3).

Integrating Policy Deployment with Xerox's Business Planning Process

To exemplify the evolution of Xerox's Leadership Through Quality process, the following material, presented by Leo (1994), provides further insights and details on the integration of policy deployment with Xerox's strategic planning process:

> After 15 years of Leadership Through Quality at Xerox, one might ask why there is a continuing need for quality. Early on, David T. Kearns, then Chairman and CEO of Xerox, offered some insight into this question when he said: "This is a race without a finish line." While Xerox has made great strides, the world we live in continues to change at an accelerating pace, and we can succeed only if we continue to focus on quality and use our quality strategy to improve our business performance.
>
> Paul A. Allaire, current Xerox Chairman and CEO, has recently pinpointed the challenge: "We are facing a 'crisis of opportunity.' On the one hand, we see attractive markets, and we have superior technology. On the other hand, we won't be able to take advantage of this situation unless we can overcome cumbersome, functionally driven bureaucracy and use our quality process to become more productive."
>
> The approach that Xerox has taken to realize the vision inherent in our "crisis of opportunity" was to reengineer our operational definition and management process for the implementation of Total Quality Management companywide. Today the Xerox 2000 Leadership Through Quality Strategy and Management Model are the means by which a corporate business excellence process is implemented annually across the corporation on a worldwide basis. Our objective is to use a companywide quality assessment and certification process, in combination with our Policy Deployment Process called "Managing For Results," to achieve world-class productivity as the key enabler to capture market opportunities.

LEADERSHIP THROUGH QUALITY EVOLUTION

The beginnings of the quality movement at Xerox can be traced to our Japanese subsidiary, Fuji Xerox. In 1976, Yotaro "Tony" Kobyashi (then president of Fuji Xerox) began the quality journey by introducing the principles and tools of total quality management, advocated by the Japanese Union of Scientists and Engineers (JUSE), to help the people of Fuji Xerox improve the company's competitive position. This effort resulted in the people of Fuji Xerox receiving the Deming Prize in 1980 and in making many improvements in its business. Examples of these improvements included a doubling of product reliability, a one-half reduction in machine cost, a one-half reduction in time-to-market, a three-quarter reduction in machine size, and a dramatic increase in copy quality as perceived by the customer.

Meanwhile, business problems in the rest of the Xerox family were becoming apparent on a worldwide basis. The early 1980s were a time of intense business pressure. Market Share and Return On Assets (ROA) declined. Over 20,000 jobs were eliminated, and employee satisfaction dropped as people began to lose confidence in senior management.

During 1982, CEO David Kearns had been witnessing firsthand the implementation of Total Quality Management (TQM) at Fuji Xerox. Kearns believed three key factors made the Japanese better than their U.S. competitors: Cost, Quality, and Expectations. Kearns noticed that the Japanese set much higher expectations for their performance and output than the United States operations did.

At about the same time, several of Kearns's key advisors suggested the use of a TQM approach to address our fundamental business problems. To put this recommendation into action, Kearns commissioned 11 senior managers to explore and outline a TQM approach for Xerox. This design team would draft a "vision book" that would project how the company would look if TQM efforts were successful. The intent was to construct a strategy and implement a plan whose impact would be broad enough and deep enough to turn the competitive tide.

As a result of this effort, the management team decided in 1983 to implement the Xerox approach to TQM, Leadership Through Quality, on a worldwide basis. It took four years to train over 100,000 people worldwide to ensure a common understanding and approach to quality at all Xerox facilities.

During the four-year deployment period, Xerox had to weather continued downward trends and business pressures, but the effort paid off. In addition to being a strategy for change within Xerox, Leadership Through Quality was a tool for measuring progress in business improvement. By 1987, the people of Xerox had reversed the decline in market share and ROA. The majority of Xerox employees had been trained—and were using—Leadership Through Quality in their daily work processes.

COMPANYWIDE QUALITY ASSESSMENT

Xerox came to understand the importance of periodic assessments in order to provide an opportunity for reflection and to stimulate future initiatives. The key to business success, after all, was in the reinforcement of both the commitment and the pursuit of continuous improvement.

The first quality assessment at Xerox was conducted in 1987, initiated by Paul Allaire after he became president of the company. The purpose of this assessment was to evaluate the progress in deployment of Leadership Through Quality, and to compare the quality results against the goals established in 1983. The objective was to measure and define gaps in quality implementation against our strategy and plan and to gain insight into why progress was not being achieved at a faster pace.

The assessment results were used by the management team to help focus on quality improvement opportunities in all areas of the company. This early work on quality assessment set the stage for the later use of the more comprehensive assessment criteria contained in the Malcolm Baldrige National Quality Award and the European Foundation for Quality Management criteria.

THE ROLE OF QUALITY AWARDS

The Xerox involvement with the world's premier quality awards has helped us formulate our approach to internal quality assessment. In order to DO things differently, we must SEE things in a different way. The assessment criteria from world-class quality awards help a company see itself from the customer point of view and to organize itself and its priorities for improvement from that point of view.

Through experience, Xerox managers have learned that periodic interventions are required to stimulate and refocus an organization engaged in a race without a finish line. Management learned that in applying for quality awards and responding to each part of the award criteria, Xerox could use the insights gained to address the gaps identified in the 1987 quality assessment. The assessment process, as specified by the various criteria for the different quality awards, proved to be an excellent business improvement tool. For instance, applying for the Deming Prize helped Fuji Xerox gain critical insights it would not have perceived otherwise. Other Xerox units, including the Netherlands, France, Britain, Canada, Mexico, and Australia, have similarly benefited.

INTEGRATING TQM WITH BUSINESS OPERATIONS

The quality award application process itself would provide a vehicle necessary for continuous improvement. By the middle of 1991, some of the senior executives at Xerox observed that the quality agenda, while influenced by the findings of various assessment activities and founded upon sound management principles, looked more like an unorganized "laundry list" than a well-structured, focused quality strategy. One member of the Allaire team suggested that Xerox needed an operational definition of Leadership Through Quality in order to put communicable meaning into the Leadership Through Quality concept.

It was also suggested that an internal worldwide Leadership Through Quality annual assessment using this definition should be integrated into the annual planning process to encourage continuous improvement. The idea behind this suggestion was to link the cycle of quality assessment and diagnosis with the resource-allocating process found within the annual operational planning process.

This linkage between policy deployment for cross-functional work process improvement activities and current business issues is the foundation of the Xerox approach to Business Excellence. The methodology allows teams of Xerox people and managers to identify the root causes for gaps in business performance and target opportunities for improvement. This identification process, in turn, guides the allocation of resources to develop and implement work process improvements.

XEROX TQM PRINCIPLES

Thus, Xerox decided to create a Management Model and internal Assessment System for Leadership Through Quality, and to position it as part of the management process that is used in the development of the annual operating plan for each unit. The following five principles guided the design of the management model and assessment methodology:

1. Fully satisfy customer-defined requirements.
2. Top management leads by example.
3. Involve, empower, and motivate employees.
4. Improve results through continuous process improvements by reducing:
   A. Variability in work process outputs.
   B. Cycle time through process improvement.
   C. Costs flowing from improvements in variability and cycle time.
5. Integrate continuous quality improvement into the daily management of the business.

XEROX OPERATIONAL DEFINITION OF QUALITY

In order to bring structure to all of the learning produced from both internal and external quality assessments, Xerox moved back to the basics and designed a model that specifies desired-state performance; assesses current state performance; and then identifies the gap between these two—focusing on the critical few actions necessary to close the gap.

Work began on this companywide quality assessment model, formally called the Xerox Management Model, in 1990. This model was designed to become the operational definition of Leadership Through Quality at Xerox. The definition of the Xerox Management Model is based on the quality principles and practices of leading experts, the Green Book (an early Xerox quality strategy document), the Baldrige Award criteria, the European Quality Award criteria, ISO 9000 criteria, and the lessons learned from the Xerox quality assessment (see Figure 6.4).

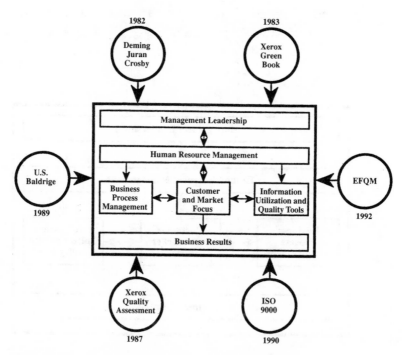

Figure 6.4 Evolution and Operation of Xerox's TQM Process Model: Leadership through Quality.

XEROX MANAGEMENT MODEL

The Xerox TQM Model identifies the six major elements of our business and how they interact with each other. (See Figure 6.5.) At the center of the model is the customer and the markets in which customers are found. The elements above and alongside the customer and market focus depict how we organize and manage ourselves to work with our customers. Our ability to focus on our customers is measured by the Business Results that we achieve.

THE VISION OF XEROX AS A WORLD-CLASS COMPANY

The model describes a vision of strong, innovative managers, who lead empowered, motivated, and challenged employees. Both managers and employees focus on the customer and continuous improvement of business processes, using the appropriate quality

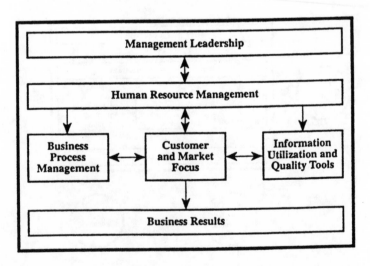

Figure 6.5 Relationships Among the Six Elements of Xerox's TQM Model.

support, information, and tools. Their efforts produce sustained and improved business results.

Each of the six categories of this Leadership Through Quality operational definition has a desired state, which is defined in terms of the vision of Xerox as a world-class company.

The six major categories in the Xerox Management Model and their desired states are described below:

1. *Management Leadership*

   Xerox management displays a customer focus, exhibits "role model behavior, establishes clear long-term goals and annual objectives, establishes strategic boundaries, and provides an empowered environment to achieve world-class productivity and business results.

2. *Human Resource Management*

   Xerox management leads, motivates, develops, and empowers people to realize their full potential. All employees are personally responsible for continuous learning and the acquisition of competencies required to achieve business objectives and to continuously improve productivity for customers and Xerox.

3. *Business Process Management*

   Business processes are designed to be customer-driven, cross-functional, and value-based. They create knowledge, eliminate waste, and abandon unproductive work, yielding world-class productivity and higher perceived service levels for our customers.

4. *Customer and Market Focus*

   Current, past, and potential customers define our business. We recognize and create markets by seeing patterns of customer requirements. Anticipating and fully satisfying those requirements through the creation of customer value achieves Xerox business results.

5. *Information Utilization and Quality Tools*

   Fact-based management is led by line management; it is achieved through accurate and timely information and by the disciplined application and widespread use of Quality tools.

6. *Business Results*

Xerox, The Document Company, is the largest and one of the most productive and profitable companies in the global documents market because:

A. Our customers' expectations are exceeded and we achieve 100% satisfaction.

B. Our people are motivated and challenged to achieve superior results for their customers.

C. We achieve optimal Market Share positions across our range of business, resulting in a premium Return On Assets.

D. We grow revenue profitably while effectively managing our cost base to achieve growth in shareholder value.

There are 42 practices that support this vision, which are organized into the six categories (this structure is informally called the "Six by Forty-two" model). Each of these practices has an identified measure that is used to assess progress toward the desired state.

TRACKING QUALITY IMPROVEMENT

This working definition of Leadership Through Quality is our guideline for measuring quality improvement from one planning cycle to another. Each of the 42 practices is evaluated on a seven-point scale. The scale ranges from a low end at level one equivalent to no demonstrable competence to the high end at level seven, representing world-class achievement. The gap between the current state and the desired state for each of these practices is used to establish priorities and to identify where effort should be placed for improvement during the next planning cycle. Specific emphasis in the operating planning process is placed on the top priorities identified during this assessment. These priorities are called the "vital few." Year-to-year progress is tracked by using the same assessment mechanism and comparing progress achieved over the prior assessments. (Figure 6.6) illustrates the Xerox companywide assessment scheme as it evolved from the initial application of

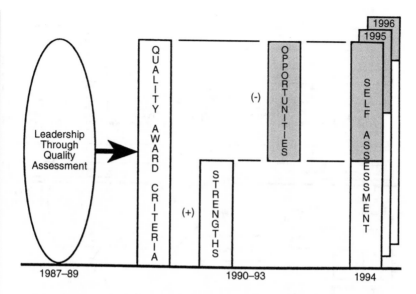

Figure 6.6 Xerox's Process for Identifying Opportunities and Tracking Performance Improvement.

Leadership Through Quality, through the quality award assessment, to the self-assessment administered by each unit in the company on a worldwide basis.

MANAGING FOR RESULTS

Xerox learned that a closed-loop planning process is essential to assuring that identified improvement goals are actually achieved. (Figure 6.7) shows in more detail how the assessment process is used to measure progress. In-process measures for each of the 42 quality practices are correlated with business results. The diagnosis of gaps in business results indicates which of the 42 practices needs attention to help close the gap and to improve business performance in the following planning cycle. These key practices are targeted as the vital few for attention when units form their operating plans for the next year.

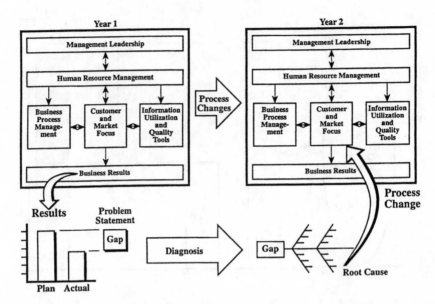

Figure 6.7 Xerox's Model for Diagnosing Performance Gaps and Driving Annual Improvements.

The policy deployment process provides the linkage between the initial diagnosis and identification of root causes for gaps, the setting of organizational objectives, and the deployment of them to the employee level. This process is called "Managing For Results" in the United States and "Policy Deployment" in both Rank Xerox and Fuji Xerox. (Figure 6.8) illustrates the major steps in this deployment process and the linkage from the corporate direction to the annual objectives of individuals. This process enhanced the Leadership Through Quality operational definition by establishing linkage between the measurement of process performance, diagnosis of performance gaps, and definition of responsibility for action to improve the process. Congruence in these steps of the planning process assures improved *alignment* between the strategic direction of the corporation and the actions of Xerox teams and individual employees. It also focuses the corporation's limited resources on the vital few strategic practices targeted for improvement.

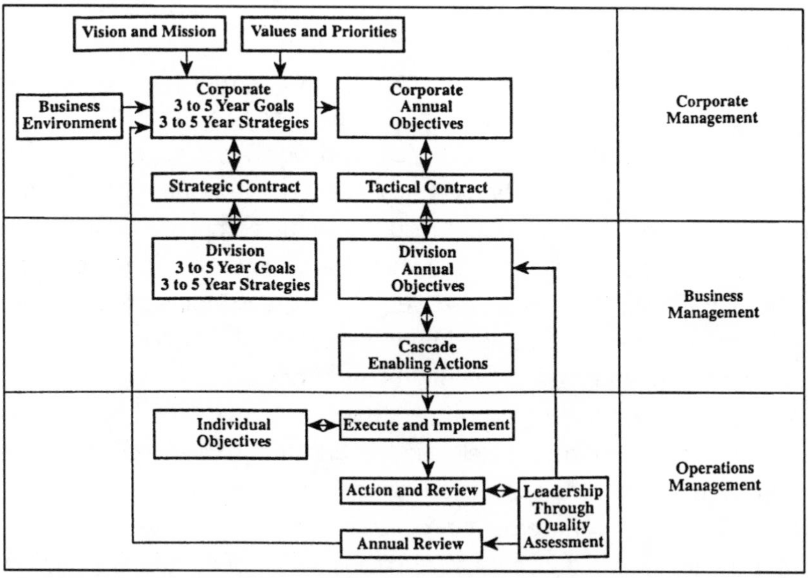

Figure 6.8 Xerox's "Managing for Results" (Policy Deployment) Process.

COMPANYWIDE QUALITY ASSESSMENT AND CERTIFICATION

In 1990, the United States Marketing Group (USMG) component of the Xerox Business Products and Systems organization decided to implement the assessment process throughout its 32,000-employee organization. During the application process for the Baldrige award, only a small subset of the total U.S. operation was examined by the Baldrige site visit team. The decision to certify all operating entities in the U.S. was made to involve all employees in the quality assessment process. The approach used was to certify each operating entity within USMG using quality assessment criteria to validate its position. To be certified, an operating unit had to achieve a minimum level of performance.

More than 140 operating entities were assessed by a team of 50 internal examiners in a series of site visits that took place from

April 1990 through June 1991. These internal examiners were members of the USMG Senior Management Team and the Corporate Quality Office. Thus, examiners became more knowledgeable and committed to TQM. The examinations revealed a range of TQM competencies. Six units achieved world-class levels of performance, while five units did not initially qualify. Units that did not certify used the assessment results to initiate improvement actions and were given follow-up site visits. Eventually, all entities were certified. Today, this baseline serves as a standard for assessing those critical few areas that need improvement within an operating unit and for measuring improvement over time.

Rank Xerox further refined this assessment methodology in 1992 for its Business Excellence Certification (BEC) Process, which is highlighted in its application for the European Quality Award.

The BEC management process enables each unit of the company to compare its own performance in all of its quality practices against an agreed set of minimum standards from the Xerox Management Model, and to make the necessary improvements to meet them over time. The results are judged by managers from other units of Rank Xerox. Achievement of the standards is formally recognized by certification. (See Figure 6.9.)

Each unit in the company is asked to assess its own performance in over 40 quality practices, which are organized into the six categories of the Xerox Management Model. Each of these practices is measured against a desired state. The resulting information is communicated to the unit and then within Rank Xerox. The management team therefore understands how each unit in the organization measures up to our standards for quality performance, and how the company as a whole is doing. The total company view is very useful to identify the systemic issues that can be targeted for breakthrough improvement.

Self-assessment is followed by a validation step: a simulated site examination that includes guidance and coaching by qualified examiners from other units. After validation comes a formal site visit and examination. If the minimum criteria are met, certification is

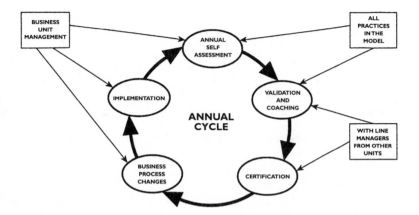

Figure 6.9 Xerox's Process for Business Excellence Certification.

awarded. The examination is also conducted by qualified examiners from other units, but not by the same units that were involved in the validation and coaching step.

The results of the assessment help shape the following year's operating plan. The BEC management process provides a detailed picture of where each unit stands, which processes need to be improved, and insights into the root causes that must be eliminated to produce improvement. It produces important customer-focused and process-based information that complements the other sources of data that go into the Policy Deployment prioritization. Another advantage of the BEC process is that it enables comparison of best practices among units. Managers are able to examine the operations of other units from across Europe and use that information to continuously improve the way they do business.

ORGANIZATIONAL REFLECTION AND LEARNING

The intensive learning gained from the Baldrige and other quality award experiences was refined into a cohesive process for assessment and improvement (see Figure 6.10). This process yields

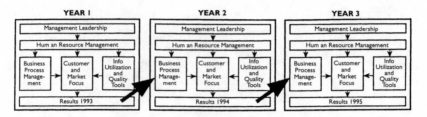

Figure 6.10 Using the Xerox TQM Model to Drive Yearly Performance Improvement.

> continuous improvement in a defined set of vital few areas in every Xerox unit, each aligned to defined corporate goals and objectives. The corporate goals themselves are aligned to serve the customers in the markets where we compete.
>
> We have used what we have learned over the past 15 years about Total Quality Management to position ourselves as The Document Company Xerox: with the goal of becoming one of the most productive and profitable companies in the global document market.

Multiple organizations have reported on using a strategic planning process based on a policy deployment process similar to Xerox's. For example, Whitaker (1993) reported on the evolution of the strategic planning process used by Arkansas Eastman to align its priorities with those of its parent company, Eastman Chemical Company. Among the reported lessons learned from Arkansas Eastman's development of its strategic planning process were:

1. A clearly defined mission effectively deployed is the foundation of an effective strategic planning process.

2. Critical elements of the business must be identified and measured as a means of determining how well you are meeting your mission and the needs of your customers.

3. Motivation stems from one's ability to see oneself in the future; therefore, a clearly defined vision is necessary for understanding and buy-in.

4. A comprehensive strategic planning process requires input from many sources. Input must be in the form of data that can be analyzed to identify improvement opportunities.

5. An organization cannot work on an unlimited number of improvement projects at the same time; however, it is vital for units to have the freedom of selection.

6. Buy-in and acceptance of the plan are greatly enhanced by early participation in the process.

7. Realistic goal setting for the organization can best be achieved through the "catchball" process.*

8. The plan–do–check–act cycle must be an integral part of the process.

9. The process should be reviewed at the beginning of every cycle to identify improvement opportunities.

Integrate Phase: Roles and Responsibilities of Upper Managers

Figure 6.11 summarizes the roles and responsibilities for upper managers throughout the Integrate Phase.

---

* "Catchball" is the term used to describe the process of alternating the deployment, review, and redeployment of goals and resources requirements via "top-down" and "bottom-up" communication. In Figure 6.2, the Catchball process is depicted via the use of the *bidirectional* arrows between corporate goals, annual business plans, unit goals, and plans operating. In Figure 6.8, the Catchball process is represented by the *bidirectional* arrows between corporate management and business management, as well as between operations management and the individuals within operations.

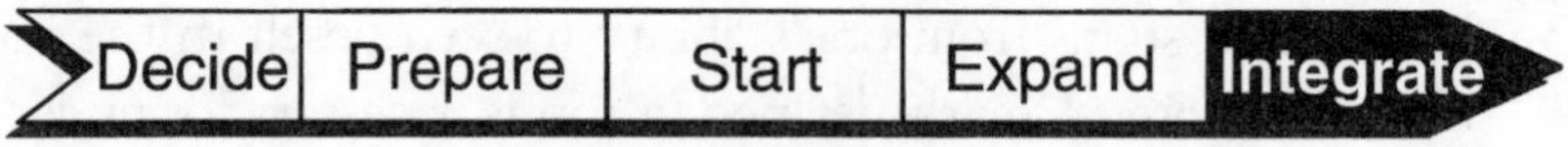

| Decide | Prepare | Start | Expand | Integrate |

Tasks for Upper Management

- Integrate quality goals into business plan.
- Deploy action to units and cross-functional teams.
- Personally conduct critical audits.
- Act on audits of quality systems.
- Continue to assess quality culture, and act on gaps.
- Integrate cross-functional process measures and results.
- Mandate unit quality assessments.
- Mandate and support training for all.
- Enable full employee participation with training and resources.
- Place upper management in full self-control.
- Expand personal participation in quality.

Figure 6.11   Tasks for Upper Managers: Integrate Phase.

Note that the word "mandate" is now used to denote the requirement that all departments/units assess, improve, and control their key departmental/unit processes (via the use of Quality for Work Groups or some similar approach).

HIGHLIGHTS OF CHAPTER 6

1. The development of a quality system infrastructure for accelerating and perpetuating performance improvements results in:

   a. Stretch goals (from benchmarking or quality assessments) for multiple dimensions of organizational performance; e.g., financial, customer satisfaction, employee satisfaction, quality.

b. Identification of key business processes and goals (via business process management).

c. Identification of departmental/functional goals (via Quality for Work Groups).

d. Identification of goals for individual employees (via Quality for Work Groups, controllability studies, and performance planning).

e. Regular reviews and audits of actual performance against the goals (e.g., via Baldrige/European Quality Reviews, audits, performance reviews).

2. Policy deployment is a key process for ensuring that the organization's strategy is communicated and truly reflected by its annual business plan.

3. Policy deployment results in identifying the "vital few" programs, processes, or projects required to *implement* an organization's strategy.

4. Policy deployment results in aligning goals and resources at all levels of the organization (corporate, division, business process, department/function, and individual) to support the "vital few" processes and projects.

5. Xerox (as well as other National Quality Award winners) has successfully used policy deployment to align its organization's goals and resources with its vision, mission, values, and business strategy within the context of its business planning process.

References

Juran, J. (1989). *Juran on Leadership for Quality*, Free Press, New York, NY.

Leo, R. (1994). "A Corporate Business Excellence Process," *Proceedings Juran Institute's IMPRO Conference*, Juran Institute, Wilton, CT.

Whitaker, A. (1993). "Strategic Planning and Alignment: The Senior Manager's Role in Total Quality Management," *Proceedings Juran Institute's IMPRO Conference*, Juran Institute, Wilton, CT.

Young, B., and Lorentz, N. (1993). "The Use of Core Process Management in the Deployment of Total Quality Management at U S WEST Communications," *Proceedings Juran Institute's IMPRO Conference*, Juran Institute, Wilton, CT.

Index

353

London Life, London T-005
HR Training & Education
Implementing Juran's road map for
quality leadership
June 12, 2006